Te s

Sex and Relationships

An A–Z guide for young Christians

Nick Harding

kevin mayhew

kevin mayhew

First published in Great Britain in 2008 by Kevin Mayhew Ltd
Buxhall, Stowmarket, Suffolk IP14 3BW
Tel: +44 (0) 1449 737978 Fax: +44 (0) 1449 737834
E-mail: info@kevinmayhewltd.com

www.kevinmayhew.com

9 8 7 6 5 4 3 2 1 0

ISBN 978 1 84867 109 6
Catalogue No. 1501147

Cover design by Rob Mortonson
Edited by Katherine Laidler
Typeset by Richard Weaver

Printed and bound in Great Britain

Introduction

Life is tough enough if you're a teenage girl! You've got all the problems of growing up and making decisions. Then there's all the pressure, education, information, rumours, looking good, boasting and stress about getting into sex and relationships.

You may be one of many young people who say they haven't learned much from sex education at school. You may have found it embarrassing, thought it was all a bit biological, or giggled all the way through! You may have thought that it said nothing about love, romance and boyfriends.

Sex is all around us – it is used to sell us anything from perfume to cars, and TV and magazines suggest that everyone has really active sex lives. Meanwhile, it is normal for you to be fancying boys and wanting to spend time with that special lad in particular! Relationships with boys can be really great – one of the joys of growing up. But when is the right time to get into having a boyfriend, what are boys like, and what's really important? In this book we're looking at the whole area of relationships and sex, unpacking it in clear and blunt detail, and asking what God, who made us, thinks about it. You'll know about some of this stuff, but you may never have thought about it in relation to your Christian faith.

So read on and think through what we have here. It could change your thinking for the better – not just for these teenage years, but for life!

Nick Harding

Aa

Advice

There is a great deal of advice on sex and relationships available, but you need to weigh it all up and think how it relates to your attitudes and what God expects of you. There are lots of websites, booklets and DVDs that give info on relationships and sex, and there are counsellors and teachers who are more than happy to listen and offer advice.

Your friends and peers at school, youth group and church will always be willing to offer you their advice too. Some of it may be worth thinking about, but they've probably not got much more experience than you and may not be offering you the best advice around!

The big problem with the huge amount of advice available is that it's hard to know what is true, what is correct, what comes from a basis that ignores the Christian faith, and what is really bad stuff! The adults at your church or youth group may be the best people to talk to and ask advice from, as they will understand a bit more about how God wants us to live.

If you're thinking about relationships and have questions about sex, then you should always get advice before doing anything. It is so easy to get carried away and dive into things that you could regret for the rest of your life.

This book is full of advice too, and I hope you enjoy reading it and take the advice here. But ultimately it is up to you!

Abortion

see Termination

Abstinence

see also Precious, Sexually Transmitted Diseases, Young

This simply means to choose not to do something, take something or take part in something. When it comes to getting into heavy petting and sexual activity, this is a great choice for many girls as well as boys. There are many Christian young people, and many other young people who are not believers, who have made a conscious and intelligent decision to keep sex until the proper place of marriage, and they stick to it. This doesn't mean that they don't have boyfriends or girlfriends and they don't have fun – in fact, many will say they feel a lot happier and freer in their relationship because there's no pressure, no hidden desires and no risks of going too far and ending up with a disease or a pregnancy.

Abstinence is strongly promoted in some countries, including the USA, while much of Europe tends to assume that all young people will have sex so they might as well be fully informed about having safe sex. There are lots of reasons why sex outside a long-term committed relationship can't ever be described as safe and the risks can be very high. Girls who choose the abstinence way are a fantastic example to their friends and they are also protecting themselves. Abstinence until the right time in the right relationship covered in love is the safest and best decision, made by thinking, brave and independent young people. Are you one?

Activities

see also Boys' Interests, Emotions, Love, Privacy, Young

When you're in a special relationship with a boy you'll want to spend time together. There are lots of things you can do together that will help you get to know him and enjoy being in each other's company.

If you don't already know what he's into, you'll need to find out, and be willing to learn a bit about his hobbies and pastimes. In the same way he will need to be willing to spend time with you while you're doing what you enjoy. You may share a sport you can both play, interest in the living world and countryside, rock music, or clubs and organisations.

If God is important to you (and I really hope God is!), then you really need to find a boy who shares your faith and has that in common with you. (It is easy to think that you can encourage a lad to come to church with you if you start going out, but in reality this rarely succeeds!) The activities and meetings at church and youth group will be another way to spend time together.

You will also want to spend time alone with your boyfriend, and there's nothing wrong with that as long as you know yourself well enough to have self-control, to know to say 'no' clearly if necessary, and not to get into physical stuff that carries all sorts of risks. A rather tacky way to help is to imagine Jesus is physically with you and your boyfriend at all times, and only do what you don't mind Jesus seeing! Odd idea, but it can help!

Adolescence

see also Boys' Bits, Embarrassment, Girls' Bits, Hormones

Adolescence is the time when things start to change in your body and your emotions. Your hormones make these changes happen, and they're the fairly obvious things such as breasts growing, spots and zits, longer legs, and hair under your arms and in your pubic area.

Adolescence is a really tough time, because as well as all the physical changes you'll also probably feel angry and knotted up inside for no reason. You'll want to be treated like an adult and have more say in your decisions and more freedom. You'll also want the security and love of home, but won't know how to ask for it! You'll want more of your own space and some privacy. Your parents or carers will be a bit confused by your moodiness and unpredictability, and you're likely to get into rows and shouting matches at home. The good news is that some of this emotional stuff and internal anger is worse for boys than for you!

Adolescence is also the time when you start to feel things emotionally for others, usually boys, that you've not felt before. You'll blush or shiver when the boy you fancy walks past or is mentioned by a friend, and you'll find it all a bit confusing! This is a time you've got to go through . . . it's how God made it to be!

Adultery

see also Divorce, Heartbreak, Lies, Marriage, Rejection, Trust

You'll probably have heard of this. It is mentioned in one of the Ten Commandments in the Bible and it's something God really wants us to avoid because it is not best for his people.

Adultery is when one person in a marriage decides to have a sexual relationship with someone else. But, as we know, having a sexual relationship with someone is a really important, deep and trusting thing to do, so if it goes wrong, it can create huge problems. This is one of the main causes of marriages ending, and it's such a shame that more people don't follow what God says!

Marriage is a very special thing, and it is within the marriage that sexual activity takes place. In a marriage the two people commit themselves to love and care for the other all the time and in every situation and to give to each other totally. If one person then goes off and gives him or herself to someone else, it often causes damage that can't be repaired.

Some marriages have survived the man or woman committing adultery, but it takes lots of hard work and determination as the trust is built up again.

Age

see also Dating, Men, Sexual Abuse

Because boys tend to develop a little later than girls and can appear very immature, you could find yourself attracted to an older boy or man. You'll think the lads of your age in your class at school or in the youth group seem childish, but older ones seem to be more grown-up and have more to offer.

There's a risk here because older boys may have more experience in relationships and may have learned how to manipulate girls and get what they want from them. There are some men who deliberately target teenage girls because of a sexual attraction to them, and this can lead to sexual abuse.

It could be that age is no problem, and as you get older any age gap seems unimportant. But while you're still in your teens you need to be really careful about these older, mature guys who pay you attention. Think carefully before you go into a relationship with them and keep asking God what he thinks.

AIDS

see also Sexually Transmitted Diseases

You will know about this already. You should also know that the only way you can catch the HIV virus is through body fluids. You can't catch it by using a loo seat, touching clothes, kissing or hugging.

AIDS is a serious world illness passed on through sexual activity, blood or by using dirty needles in drug-taking. People with the HIV virus pass it on to others, and although it can be controlled by drugs, many people die of AIDS-related illnesses. It is not God's intentional judgement on a world that ignores him, but it is a result of a world that doesn't follow God's advice. In many African countries, where AIDS is a major problem, the only way to avoid it is to avoid any sexual activity until adulthood and ensure that the sexual partner has done the same.

'Safe' sex – using a condom – is promoted as the best way to avoid the HIV virus and AIDS, yet condoms can go wrong. The only really safe way to avoid it is to keep sex to permanent relationships, God's ideal being marriage.

Appearance

see also Attraction, Precious, Self-Worth

How you look is going to become increasingly important to you as you grow up, but it isn't everything! You may try to attract boys by being clean and wearing fashionable clothes or choosing a new hairstyle that's going to catch the eye. It is really good to take pride in how you look, and if you do manage to turn a boy's head, then all the better! But comparing yourself to your friends and other girls at school or college can get a bit competitive, and that can be harmful. You're not in a competition to look like someone else . . . you are you!

Appearance is only one thing about someone. You could look really attractive but have a cruel or selfish personality! The same goes for boys. Boys will find you attractive because of your hair, your smile or your breasts, but your personality is much more important. You will find a lad attractive if he's got a good figure, nice bum or great smile, but that's not all he is! You don't want to be going out with a boy who looks great but treats you really badly or is always taking and never giving. Appearance is important and you're right to be concerned about it. But, as God reminds us, it's better to look at the inside of someone as well as the outside!

Attraction

see also Boys, Boys' Bits, Crush, Desire, Heartbreak, Love

No one really knows what attracts one person to another. There are attractive things about boys but not all girls will fancy the same boy. Boys will look at you and your friends and they won't all fancy the same girl. That's what attraction is all about!

When you are attracted to a boy you will know it, because you'll feel a bit nervous and confused. You may go off your food, want to look more sexy or attractive, and think through ways of getting into conversation with him. The great thing is that if he's attracted to you, he'll be going through the same feelings and have the same worries about what to do next. Your friends may offer advice, but you shouldn't always do what they say because you don't want to get it wrong.

The only way to find out whether the attraction is going to lead to a closer friendship is to act on it by talking to him. These days you don't have to wait for the boy to make the first move! If he rejects you, it'll be tough, but then at least you know where you stand and you can move on. If he's keen, then take it slowly and see where it goes.

Attraction is often about how someone looks, and once you get to know him you may decide that he doesn't have an attractive personality and maybe simply wants to count you as one of his 'conquests'. If you're not sure, then it's best to move on . . . gently and tactfully, of course.

Bb

Bedrooms

see also Activities, Desire, Privacy

What does it look like? What does it say to others about you? I guess it's probably a bit girly, comfortable and a special place for you to be. Your bedroom is your space, where you can do your own thing and keep your belongings. It's somewhere to go to when you want some time on your own, when you've had a row, when you want to pray or think, or when you want to do something in private.

It is great to have your own space and be able to invite friends into it and keep away from parents or younger brothers and sisters. It's important for you to have that privacy and space to hang out safely. But even your bedroom is risky! It's not the best place to take your boyfriend if you're tempted to get into kissing and touching, as the privacy makes you feel safer and the bed is a great place to lie together. All too easily that can lead to you getting into stuff you both know you shouldn't.

If you want to spend time alone with a boy in your bedroom, put things on the bed to avoid the temptation to lie on it, keep the door slightly open so that you can be disturbed more easily, and, if you really can't control yourself or know that he can't, stay downstairs instead!

Bible, Sex and Relationships

The Bible has lots of things to say about relationships and sex, and there are many Christians and others who study it and have strong and differing views on what it all means! Some say that what the Bible says was written for readers 2000 years ago or more and is not as important now, while others think that the Bible's rules remain true today and should be followed to make life happier and better.

God wants people to be happy and he wants us to have friends and a range of people we can turn to for help and support. There are lots of examples of people who are close friends and not pairing off into girlfriend-boyfriend relationships. God's plan is that sex takes place between a man and a woman within marriage. The Bible says that God is unhappy about men sleeping with other men, and many people would see this as meaning women and women too and that the passage applies to all humankind. The Bible also criticises anyone doing sexual acts with animals and people breaking their marriage vows by adultery. But some people argue about those Bible passages and disagree with them. God doesn't approve of people selling their bodies to others for sex and expects everyone to respect others.

God forgives anyone who goes wrong and makes a mess of things, and his plan is that we're happy by sticking to the things he knows will keep us happy. If you want to know more about what the Bible says and what your church thinks about the Bible's teachings on relationships, talk to a leader.

Bible Passages

During the time the Bible was written people lived in many different ways and some of the traditions were immoral and dangerous, so the Bible tries to help people discover the right way to live.

God rates marriage. The first explanation of marriage comes right at the start of the Bible in Genesis 2:24, and the Bible says it should be honoured and respected in Hebrews 13:4. The importance of a good marriage and sex within marriage is highlighted in Proverbs 5:18-20 and 1 Corinthians 7:3-5.

There are loads of warnings against getting into sexual activity and appeals to keep ourselves pure for God. Have a look at 1 Corinthians 6:13, Romans 13:13 and 1 Corinthians 6:18. These passages were written to Christians and are based on the laws that God set down in the Old Testament.

There are two brief mentions of homosexual activity and how God feels about it in Romans 1:27 and Leviticus 18:22. But some Christians say that a short verse about David and Jonathan's friendship in 2 Samuel 1:26 suggests that they had a gay relationship, and there is no specific mention of women in gay relationships.

The Old Testament book Song of Songs, sometimes called Song of Solomon, is a series of love poems from a man to a woman and replies from the woman to the man, and shows what love and desire can be about. Jews say that this is a picture of God's relationship with his people, and

Christians think it's about the relationship between Jesus and the Church.

If you think you are in love with a boy, or that he is in love with you, compare your relationship and attitudes to each other with what the famous passage in 1 Corinthians 13 says. If your love is like that, your relationship is going to go places!

There's loads more that the Bible has to teach us about respect for other people, love, trust, caring – and passion too! If you want to know more, get a Bible concordance or a Bible dictionary, or talk to a youth leader or church leader.

Bisexual

see also Forgiveness, Gay, Heterosexual, Lesbian

A person who calls themself 'bisexual' is attracted to both males and females, so a bisexual girl will fancy other girls and will fancy boys too. This is a confusing situation for anyone to be in, and it's not easy for others to understand.

As teenage boys develop and get used to their changing bodies and confusing emotions, some will go through a 'gay' phase, and others will find that they fancy both girls and other boys. This can also happen to girls as you look up to older girls and women. This can be part of growing up for many and isn't usually acted upon before it passes, which it usually does. It is not in God's plan that people should be confused by their own sexual identity. We are designed physically and emotionally to be attracted to the opposite gender, and if we feel confused, we need to get help and talk to others about it. God really does understand how you feel if you're in this situation.

Boyfriends

see also Boys, Boys as Friends, Men, Valentine's Day

Look, there's no rush! You are not in a race to be the first girl in the youth group to have a boyfriend, and it's not always as good as you imagine anyway.

But when you feel your stomach churn and you're a bit embarrassed in his presence, it's possible that the time has come to ask a boy out or show him that you're interested by talking to him and making eye-contact. Then you'll need to be ready for rejection, or even know how to control yourself if he says 'Yes'!

If all goes well and you get your lad, be careful – they are delicate and so are you. Your boy should look after you really well, do nothing to upset you and make sure that you are happy. He should never force you into anything, threaten violence or hurt you.

Don't rush into snogging – let time pass and get to know each other first. Don't spend every last penny on his Valentine's Day present but do get him a nice card. Don't manipulate his feelings or treat him as if he doesn't matter – that's just not fair. And remember that, while it's unlikely that he's the boy you will end up spending the rest of your life with, he is at least willing to put up with you for a while, and that can't be bad!

Boys

see also Attraction, Boyfriends

Boys develop more slowly than girls and go through loads of changes and challenges at the same time as you do, and it's pretty rotten for them to be teenagers. Part of becoming a man means that they will feel they've got to be brave and strong, but that's usually hiding real insecurity and fear. They also worry about relationships, spots, self-image, weight, willy size and the other problems that life throws their way. Because they mature more slowly than you and can seem childish and silly, you're likely to look down on the boys your age and instead fancy older boys and men teachers!

But boys are designed to be attractive to you. They've got muscles, faces and hair, bums and bodies that you like the look of. It's natural, it's right and it's good to like the look of the males of the species!

Boys as Friends

see also Boyfriends, Friends, Precious, Young

Lots of girls are really good friends with boys, and that friendship relationship can be better than having an exclusive boyfriend. Having a number of friends who are lads is really helpful – you can learn about boys from them and they can give you advice when you decide to ask a lad out. You may find that one of your friends who is a boy becomes a bit more interesting to you, and that friendship can develop into a girlfriend-boyfriend relationship.

Friends are important to us all, and it doesn't really matter whether your best and closest friends are boys or girls. It is a much more healthier way to learn about boys than jumping into a one-to-one relationship before you're ready.

Boys' Bits

see also Girls' Bits, Impotence, Sexual Arousal

Boys go through physical changes in their teenage years, and their emotions get messed up as well as their bodies while they are growing into men. Most of their bits are in their pants . . . and best kept there! So here's a list of what they've got and what it does.

Penis (prick, willy, dick, etc.): Their penis is muscle that becomes erect and stands up hard when it fills with blood vessels, often when they're thinking about love and sex. Sometimes it seems to have taken on a life of its own and become erect for no apparent reason. Most boys ease the pressure by masturbating sometimes. When not erect, boys' penises will vary in size and some boys will be very conscious of this. Once excited and erect, they are all about the same size. Some girls find that a penis is attractive, but others think it's rather odd!

Sperm: This is a thick, creamy white liquid that the penis produces when a lad is sexually excited. One of the millions of sperm he produces can fertilise an egg in a girl, causing a pregnancy and therefore creating a new life!

Testicles (balls, etc.): The two round balls under the penis are where sperm is made and comes from when a boy ejaculates. The scrotum is the loose skin bag that his testicles are in.

Boys' Interests

see also Activities, Give and Take

Boys are not all interested in the same things and every lad is different . . . if you've not discovered that yet, you soon will! From the beginning, when we have the story of God creating man and woman to be different from each other, their behaviour and interests have been different. But there are some things that most boys will be interested in.

As they get older, boys become increasingly concerned about how they look and what they wear. They are likely to want to wear clothes that have the right labels on them and that are in fashion with their mates. Boys may be concerned about how they look and worry about their weight. An increasing number of boys also develop eating disorders.

Lads are often really into sport, both watching it and playing it. Rugby, football and cricket can dominate their brains and their time, and it can take a strong girl to drag them away from the TV when a footy match is on! The other things boys may be into include cars, horror movies, mechanics, engineering, war and battles, and anything that is noisy and messy! Like you, they'll be into music, films and TV, but are more likely to go for heavy stuff than girls. As you develop your relationship with your boyfriend, you'll need to go along with some of these things sometimes, even though you'd rather be listening to slightly more gentle music or watching a TV show.

Boys are not as likely to take schoolwork and their future careers as seriously as you, and they can lag behind a bit. In many boy-girl relationships girls can help boys settle to schoolwork and do their best, which is always a good thing.

The boy you rate as special will have other interests that make them unique, and you may share some of those. This is a great opportunity to learn about new things and to enjoy stuff that you knew nothing about. Support him and he's likely to support you in your hobbies too.

Bras

see also Attraction, Boys, Girls' Bits

Once your breasts start developing you'll be very aware of them – and perhaps a little embarrassed! Bras are designed to offer support as well as to cover them up a bit! Wearing a bra for the first time is a big step – it shows that you're growing up. Of course, some silly little boys may find it funny, but ignore them. There are patterned bras, bras designed to add extra support when playing sport, and bras designed to make your breasts look bigger or more attractive to the male of the species!

Many women have back and neck problems because they wear bras that don't fit properly. It may seem a bit scary at the time, but it's best to go to a shop where understanding women can help you get the right size for you, and make sure your mum or another woman you trust helps you.

Bum

see also Boys' Bits, Girls' Bits

It's never been fully understood why the bum, whose main purpose is to get rid of excess junk from the body, is attractive to both men and women! Our bum shape is generally not within our control, although eating too much or not enough affects the fat on the bum.

Lads' bums can seem attractive, and you might have looked at some boys and thought that yourself. You may also worry about your bum looking big. But there's nothing to worry about – when you choose the right lad for you and he chooses you, what your bum looks like will not be important!

Cc

Certificate 18

see also Law, Pornography, Precious, Young

These are films and DVDs that are considered by others to be unsuitable for anyone under the age of 18 to watch. They may contain a great deal of horror, have themes about abuse and rape, violence, mutilation and death, or contain graphic scenes of sexual activity. You've probably seen films that are unsuitable, and you may have been scared or thrilled by the experience.

There are good reasons why films have age warnings on them. Despite how it seems, it is not a case of adults wanting to keep secrets or be spoilsports. Decisions on 'Certificate 15' and 'Certificate 18' films are made by groups of people who understand the damage that inappropriate scenes can cause in the minds of teenagers. They have to draw the line somewhere, or even very young children would be allowed to watch things that would damage them.

Sexual scenes and themes of films can give warped and wrong impressions of what relationships are like. It's worth remembering that just because a film shows it, it doesn't make it right, normal or good. For instance, romantic films suggest that it's all going to be lovely in the end, but real life isn't always like that!

Boys can get a thrill from films that show sexual scenes and may want to get you to watch them to get you excited. Don't be fooled by their reasons and do what you know is right.

Chat Rooms

see also Internet Dangers, Paedophiles, Sexual Abuse

Going on to internet chat rooms can be a great way to find out how other people like you are getting on with life and to share your thoughts without anyone judging you. You may make friends with others and offer them help as well as getting help from them. But chat rooms have their dangers too. Some of the people you meet in a chat room may be giving really rubbish advice, so you should think about it carefully and weigh it up with what others say. Also you don't actually know who it is you're communicating with, and some users may be older than they say and possibly dangerous too.

There have been a number of cases where older men who are attracted to teenage girls have used chat rooms to befriend girls and arrange to meet them in order to sexually assault or abuse them. Many teenage girls use the web as a network of friendships, so this is a risk you must be careful about.

You should always be careful not to give too many personal details to anyone in a chat room. You may decide to use a false name and you should never give your address or other stuff that could lead to you being traced. Adults who use chat rooms in order to get to know young people and abuse them are really good at pretending and covering up their true identity, so never agree to meet up with people you only know through the chat room.

Contraception

see also Abstinence, Bible, Pregnancy, Sexually Transmitted Diseases

There are a number of forms of contraception and most of you will know about these in some detail because taking pills or having things fitted to a girl's body is something that happens to you, and not to boys.

The cap or diaphragm is a small disc of plastic that fits inside a girl's vagina and stops sperm reaching her womb.

The coil is a small piece of plastic, sometimes with metal too, that fits inside the womb, preventing the sperm from reaching an egg and also affecting the lining of the womb and making it less likely to accept a fertilised egg.

The 'pill' is a tablet which causes a change in the hormones of a girl or woman and stops eggs being produced. The 'morning-after pill' does something similar and has to be taken within three days of sexual intercourse. The earlier it is taken, the more likely it is to work.

The 'rhythm method' is a way of working out the times each month when a girl is most likely to be producing eggs. The couple avoids having sex during those times.

This is not always very reliable because many girls do not have 'regular' periods.

The condom is a rubber sheath that fits over a boy's erect penis and stops the sperm spilling out into the girl's womb. Condoms are not comfortable and not totally reliable as they can split. Some statistics suggest that when used by teenagers, up to 30 per cent of condoms fail.

Some people suggest that a boy can avoid making a girl pregnant by withdrawing his penis just before he ejaculates, but this is full of risks. His penis may let out a little sperm while inside the girl, and in the heat of the moment it may simply be impossible for him to come out at the right time.

The best way for any girl or woman to avoid creating an unwanted pregnancy and all the pain that it causes is to avoid full sexual intercourse until you are settled with your life-partner.

Some boys take the attitude that they don't have to take responsibility, but that's rubbish! What you do with a boy and what you allow him to do could have huge consequences, and you have to be willing to take responsibility too.

There's a lot of pressure put on young people to use contraception, particularly condoms, because they avoid pregnancy and can help stop the spread of sexually transmitted diseases. But just because they're available, it doesn't mean that you should use them. If you use contraception, you're likely to get into sexual activity earlier than you're emotionally ready for, and because of that you could feel cheated, used and abused. Many girls and some boys feel rejected and worthless if they become sexually active and get through a number of partners. And in the future when you do meet your lifelong partner you won't be able to enjoy the fullness of sexual activity and discovery with them, as you'll have been there before.

Contraception is not always approved of by Christians. God designed us to get into sexual activity within marriage, and part of that is to produce children. Contraception by all these methods, apart from the rhythm method, involves a physical or chemical way to stop the sperm from connecting with an egg and creating life, and some would say that is close to killing a potential child.

Make time to pray about this, and talk to an older Christian you trust before getting into anything that you'll regret later.

Crush

see also Desire, Rejection, Young

A 'crush' is a bit of a cheap word to describe something that can take up all your time and your thinking! The song 'Stacy's Mom' by the pop group Fountains of Wayne is all about a crush a boy has on a woman. In it a boy hangs out with his friend Stacy, but really he fancies her mum and spends his time thinking and dreaming about her. He knows it can come to nothing, but still he has that crush on her.

You may find that your mind becomes obsessed with some guy who you know deep down is unreachable and not likely to be interested in you. You may develop a crush on a young male teacher, the dad or older brother of one of your friends, or even an older girl. A crush can become a bit of an obsession and can cause you to do embarrassing things that are best avoided. People who have crushes have been known to follow their 'victim', buy them unwanted presents or leave them really inappropriate notes! Difficult as it is, it's best to be really tough on yourself and realise as soon as possible that it is a waste of your time and energy. Better to look out for fit boys of your own age instead.

Curiosity

see also Boyfriends, Boys, Desire, Young

There's nothing wrong with being curious, and with sex and relationships so obvious in advertising, TV, magazines and films, you're likely to be curious about those things too. You'll want to find out about your own body and how it is changing, as well as thinking through what it's like to spend time with a boy, hold hands, kiss and do other things!

There's lots of info out there, but it's not all helpful. And it really isn't worth getting into stuff just because you are curious about how it feels or what happens. There are implications for everything you do on your own and for things you do when you're in a relationship with someone. You need to keep thinking about the possible pain and harm of not taking things seriously until it's too late. Be curious . . . but be controlled too. God has given us the ability to control ourselves and sometimes we need to use it!

Cyber Sex

see also Chat Rooms, Internet Dangers, Sexual Abuse

There is a growing number of really bad and unhelpful websites where, usually after paying a fee, adults engage in what's called 'cyber sex'. By typing in responses and having an on-line conversation, the people involved pretend they are in a relationship and are having sexual intercourse. Of course, the Bible was written a couple of thousand years before computers, so cyber sex doesn't feature in God's book, but there is a lot of stuff that relates to having pure minds and not thinking things that are not right. In the Gospel of Matthew (5:27-28) Jesus says that, for married men, thinking about another woman is just as wrong as actually committing adultery, and it's fair to interpret that in the same way for married women too. Some people suggest that to think about doing something is the same as actually doing it and that applies to sexual fantasies too. This sort of activity is driven by the world's obsession with sex and its neglect of the right ways to live and develop healthy relationships.

Dd

Dating *see also Boyfriends, Ending, Heartbreak*

Dating and 'going out with' are the same thing. If you are moving towards a close relationship with a particular guy, you will want to spend time with him, and the first move is often to wait for him to ask you out 'on a date', or go for it and ask him instead! This can mean going to see a film or simply coming round to your house for tea. Once you have got to know that lad a little more, you may decide that you've got nothing to talk about or that he's not as interesting as you thought, and you'll gently explain that the relationship isn't working for you. On the other hand, you might find that you really like him and he really likes you!

Dating or going out with someone is something people laugh and tease others about, yet once you're a teenager it's a really important step in your development towards becoming a fully formed woman. It's right that you have lots of friends, both boys and girls, but if you get into a relationship with a particular boy, you'll start to learn about how men tick, what they like and don't like and the things you have in common. This will help you work out the sort of man you may eventually want to marry and settle down with for life. But dating comes with a warning too! If you spend too much time with your boyfriend, your other friends will get bored with you. And you must be careful that your relationship is going at a speed that you are both really happy with. Don't let him force you into rushing things!

Desire

see also Precious, Self-Worth, Sexual Arousal

This is a strange thing! There can be lots of things we desire, from getting great marks in the exam we've done no revision for, to buying something fabulous we've seen in a magazine or on TV. Desire is described as a longing or a craving for something, and it can get us really heated up. We may believe from watching films and soaps that we can have whatever we desire, but that's not how life really is.

If you're normal, you'll probably have seen a really fit man that you desire . . . but you know that the desire can come to nothing. That's a bit like a crush and is best forgotten. Desire can be more serious than that and can make people do things that they'll look back on and cringe! You may desire things, but you have to keep the energy and passion that desire can bring in check. Desire for sex is best kept for the right man in the right relationship . . . that's one that will last.

Divorce

see also Adultery, Marriage

If you are not from a 'split' family, then it's likely that up to half of your friends are. Divorce usually comes as the result of a long period of difficulties in a marriage, and culminates in the couple splitting up and one or other moving out of the house. God didn't want it to be that way, but we live in an imperfect world full of imperfect people who make mistakes. God would like marriages to last and families to be stable and settled, but he still loves the people involved when marriages and families go wrong.

Divorce hits all kinds of families, and Christian families are not immune from marriage difficulties. For children in the middle of a divorce, it's natural to feel that they are responsible for it all in some way and caused it to happen, but this is simply not true. It's also part of the experience to take sides, yet often both sides have done things that have not helped the relationship to grow. If you are hurting after a divorce in your family, nothing is gained by hating your father, resenting your mother or blaming God that it happened in the first place.

God loves us all and wants to bring healing to all situations and pain. He can heal the memories and hurt felt by children, parents and friends involved. He can help people get over their experiences of divorce and look forward to their own successful marriage later in life.

Dumping

see also Ending, Heartbreak, Rejection

It's probably going to happen, so be ready! Being dumped is the phrase used when your boyfriend decides that he's had enough of you and wants to move on. He may already fancy another girl or he's simply got bored or found that you're not the sort of girlfriend he wants or you won't do what he wants. If the relationship really means something to you, this will be painful and may knock your confidence for a while. If you weren't serious anyway, you'll both soon bounce back. The same thing applies if you decide to move on from your boyfriend because it is not working out.

The word 'dumping' is not great! It suggests that you are rubbish and being thrown to one side. If a good relationship comes to an end and you're both being a bit grown up about it, you'll be careful and sensitive when ending. That way you'll survive the experience and probably remain friends.

Boys have a really bad reputation for dumping girls when they've had what they want from them – or when they find out they're not going to get what they want! This is a really bad, crude and cruel way of treating girls, and boys should grow up and know better! You are not for jumping into bed with or using in any way. And you're certainly not for casting aside and moving on without care or sensitivity. Likewise, you should never be treated badly by a lad who is using you to make someone else jealous or who doesn't really care about you.

Ee

Education

see also Advice, Peers, Teachers

At school you'll probably have been through a number of courses of sex education and some work on the importance of relationships too. Yet many young people like you say they didn't learn much in sex ed and in particular that it seemed a bit technical and not about meaningful relationships.

There's a big debate going on in the UK as to whether the level of under-age sexual activity and high teenage pregnancy rates are connected with the standard and frequency of sex education. Some say that too much sex ed makes young people want to get into it too soon, while others argue that the more you know, the safer you will be. This may be true, but being 'safe' physically doesn't mean that your emotions are protected or that you're really ready to give your body and deepest feelings to someone. There's so much more to relationships than you are taught at school!

Embarrassment

see also Appearance, Self-Worth

You will know what it is like to be embarrassed! You'll know that awkward blush that covers your face and you can do nothing about. You'll know that feeling when you try to speak and you can't string any words together. You'll know what it's like to want to vanish into space or to wish for a hole to open up and swallow you!

It's unavoidable that, as you grow up and start to fancy boys, you're going to get into embarrassing situations. It can be really tough to pluck up courage to show a lad that you're interested and to have to wait for him to make a move, and simply dreadful when he doesn't fancy you. Or you may be embarrassed about your body and how you compare to your friends and peers. The good thing is that, if you put it to one side and get on with life, the sense of embarrassment passes and you grow in confidence.

Embarrassment is all about what other people think of us and, as we become more confident about ourselves, it is less powerful and less awful to be embarrassed. We know that God loves us and that's the most important thing, so there's nothing to be embarrassed about. Don't let others get to you – just get on and enjoy life!

Emotions

see also Desire, Heartbreak, Love

There's nothing wrong with being emotional, and girls are much more connected with their emotions than lads are. But boys and men can show emotions too! People who know themselves well and are in tune with how they feel will be able to show their emotions. Our faith and our worship sometimes demand an emotional response as we think about all that Jesus did for us and all that it means for us now.

When you're growing up and developing into a woman, your emotions may be a bit all over the place. Sometimes you will find that things get out of hand, and feelings get blown up and become stronger than they should be. This can mean that you get really upset over things that you would normally just get a bit frustrated by, or that your emotions towards someone you fancy become a bit extreme. Your emotions can affect your judgement, and, for instance, if you are dumped, you'll take it really hard for a while and find yourself crying a lot.

You can't do much about this, but the more in touch with yourself you are, the better it will be. Make sure you have family and friends around who are willing to see you through your emotional upheavals and tell you honestly when you may be over-reacting. Sometimes our feelings will get hurt and we'll feel scarred inside for a while, but it is always better to have emotions and allow this than to hide how we feel and keep it all bottled up.

Ending

see also Dumping, Heartbreak, Lies, Precious, Rejection

There may be times when you will know it is time to stop going out with your boyfriend. He may not be all that you want in a lad, or he may want to spend time with others instead of you. You do need to think and pray carefully before you end a relationship because it is always painful both for you and the bloke involved. On the other hand, you should never feel trapped in a relationship, and if you don't think you can cope, then it's best to get out. When you're older you'll be thinking more seriously about whether you have a long-term future with the man, and then it's even more important to end it if you're not sure it is what you or God want.

Ending the relationship can be really tough, particularly as you should have grown to be very close and 'fond' (an old-fashioned word, but quite useful!) of him. He may also have developed some power over you and you could feel forced to keep the relationship going after its sell-by date! You should always try to talk about how you are both feeling and be as open and honest as you can. Be aware that you can get emotional and some boys may be manipulated by this. For instance, if he's trying to end a relationship with you, he's likely to back off and give way if you burst into tears or threaten to do something bad, and that's not honest or helpful.

Never end a relationship by email, text, SMS message, Facebook, phone message or through a friend. Instead you need to work out a way of meeting and talking where he will have support nearby and where you can get away fairly easily. Lads simply hate being dumped by a girl and it hits their pride really hard. You may find it helpful to follow up the conversation with a letter, but always try to speak to him first and be ready for his friends (and possibly yours too) to be a bit hard on you for a while.

Equality

see also Boys, Men

Girls who have lots of boyfriends in succession may suffer gossip and be accused of being cheap and 'easy', while boys who have plenty of girlfriends may be seen as really manly and mature. This is complete rubbish and shows that in some areas of relationships we have got to go a long way before girls and boys are treated rightly and equally! In a world which is much more aware of the different but equal needs and rights of all people, we must behave properly and not see boys as being in any way better or having more rights than girls.

In many cultures it is still expected for a boy to ask a girl out and to pay for any dates. But you may choose to take the lead yourself and there's nothing wrong with that!

Ff

Faith

see also Bible, Lifelong Partner, Marriage

There's a bit in the Bible about how important it was to marry people from the same race, country or religion. Much of that doesn't apply in the same way now, but if you believe in God and have a living faith, then you've got to think about the kind of people you want to spend time with . . . and possibly share your life with. In 2 Corinthians (6:14) Paul talks about being in partnership with someone else and how difficult that is if the other person does not believe what you believe. There's something really important about having a boyfriend who shares the same ideas, beliefs and attitudes as you do. A Christian teenage couple can be a great example to others and used really powerfully by God in lots of ways. This is very important when you fancy a boy and want to ask him out. Will he understand your faith and does he share it? Will you be able to pray together as well as having fun in other ways? Will he feel the same way as you about what the Bible says about sex? Will you want to spend time with him and feel yourself pulled between church, youth group and your boyfriend? Will he lead you away from church, your friends and your faith? These are questions only you can answer, but you've got to take them seriously.

There are people who came to a Christian faith through going to church with someone they liked and learning about their faith. But this is the exception rather than the rule. Many people will say that they'll come along in order to get the girl or boy they are after, but once in the relationship their attitude can change. God loves you and he wants you to be a great Christian girl and woman. There's a lot to lose if you go out with a boy who doesn't know God like you do and doesn't want to.

Foreplay

see also Petting, Sexual Arousal

You'll have heard of this but may be a bit confused about what it means and whether it is a good thing to do or not. The term is used to describe sexual activity that gets both the man and woman excited and aroused before the act of sexual intercourse takes place.

Foreplay starts with kissing, and you may already know that when you kiss deeply and for a long time you feel sexually excited, and the boy you're kissing may get an erection. Then foreplay leads on to touching, undressing, exploring each other. Foreplay is all about intimate and very personal exploration that happens in a committed, long-term relationship. Some of what we describe as foreplay is also known as petting, and there's more on this later.

Forgiveness

see also Abstinence, Bible

God is amazing . . . I hope you agree! One of the most incredible things about God is that he is always willing to forgive us when we really mean that we are sorry and when we seek his help in sorting ourselves out and not going wrong again. This isn't an excuse for doing exactly what we want to do and then turning to God – he knows how we really feel inside and whether we are genuine or not!

As you go through the difficult, stormy waters of growing up and getting into relationships and thinking about what sex really is, you may make some mistakes. You may find that in private you are getting into a bad habit of very regular masturbation, or you're looking at pornographic pictures of boys and men. You may be jealous of others, lie to your boyfriend, or get into sexual activity that he and you are not really ready for or comfortable with. All of these things will make you feel bad as your conscience kicks in and you think of all that you know about God's way to live. But nothing is beyond forgiveness. God really wants to forgive any of us who know we've got it wrong. The key thing is to ask for his forgiveness and ask for the power of the Holy Spirit to help you keep control and live a life more like what God wants of you.

Friendships *see also Boys as Friends, Peers, Young*

The Bible has many examples of really good friendships both between girls and between men and women. Jonathan and David were great friends and needed each other to get through a tough time. Ruth and Naomi set a great example of care and trust between two women. Jesus had loads of friends around him, including the disciples and some women too. There's no suggestion that Jesus had a girlfriend – but he did have many friends of both genders. You need good friends around you too, and they don't all need to be girls. Friends can help you when things go wrong in life or when you're not sure what to do. Real friends will stand by you at the toughest times and will give you good advice.

Sometimes when a girl gets a boyfriend that relationship takes over the girl's life and they no longer seem interested in their friends. This is bad news, because if the boyfriend dumps the girl, she'll be left with no one to help her and no one to talk to. Once you get into a relationship with a lad, be careful to get the right balance, spending time with him and spending time with your mates.

F Word

see also Sexual Intercourse

The F word is now widely used in TV and films, songs and in school playgrounds. People say it when things are going wrong and when they are frustrated. It no longer has the shock value that it used to, but you have got to think about the words that you say before you say them. The Bible talks of our mouths revealing what we're like inside, so if we use foul language, we're showing that we're not quite as God wants us to be.

The word relates to the basic act of sexual intercourse and is a horribly blunt and rough way to describe what God designed to be a loving, beautiful and special experience.

This act is not something you simply 'have' or 'do', because this takes away the emotional and uniquely personal nature of sex. This word cheapens something that is very precious.

Gg

Gay

see also Bisexual, Heterosexual, Lesbian, Masturbation

The word 'gay' means homosexual. A few generations ago 'gay' simply meant happy and cheerful and had no sexual connections. Later it was used as a term of criticism or insult against people who were homosexual. Boys who are into dance, art and performing may be called 'gay', although that has nothing to do with their sexuality.

A gay or homosexual boy or man is someone who is sexually attracted to another male and is not attracted in the same way to girls or women. There has been a move in recent years to ensure that men who are gay and women who are lesbian have similar rights to others, and it is illegal to discriminate against homosexuals. There is also much more media attention given to gay rights, celebrations and gay TV and music stars.

It is clear from what the Bible says that God's ideal is that men and women get together, but some people think this is no longer important and encourage gay people to worship God. It is a difficult area, and people have strong feelings on both sides. If you feel attracted to other girls, don't worry – you're not a freak, it's not unusual, and God still loves you. Many Christians think that people who are gay and lesbian should be welcomed in churches, but they shouldn't be in sexually active relationships. For your own safety it's best to avoid any sexual contact with other girls, and it would be worth talking about how you feel to an adult you trust, such as your youth group leader.

Gay Sexual Activity

see also Bible, Gay, Lesbian, Sexually Transmitted Diseases

Some young people are sexually attracted to others of the same gender as they grow up and become more aware of sexual desire, and a few will take part in teenage gay sexual activity. With two girls this will include kissing, touching and feeling.

There is a brief passage in the Bible (Leviticus 18:22) that says that God finds men having sex with other men to be wrong, and many Christians go along with that teaching and interpret it the same for women having sex with women. Others say that love is a special thing and to find love with the same gender isn't necessarily wrong. Remember that God loves everyone he made and, whatever they do, he promises to forgive and help them change. If you've been involved in gay sexual activity God doesn't hate you, but you may need help in thinking through how God really wants you to be and to act. Better to get help and advice than hide what you've done or how you feel.

Girls *see also Boyfriends, Girls' Bits, Periods, Women*

God created the female of the race to have all the things boys like – shapely figures, breasts, bums, long hair and high voices! You may or may not have all of these things, but there are still boys out there who will find you attractive!

You're going to like this – girls develop physically and emotionally earlier than boys, your brains develop earlier and you're better emotionally connected. Boys tend to be a bit dimmer and not get the hints that girls give them! Girls are great – you're one, so be proud!

Girlfriends *see also Boys, Boys as Friends, Men*

Some boys simply want to say they've got a girlfriend for the image it gives, and some think it's great to play around with two girls at once. This is simply wrong! You should never allow yourself to be used as some sort of human trophy by a boy, even if he is the one that every girl seems to fancy! Often the shy boys who are very cautious about asking girls out are the ones who are more loving, understanding, and supportive.

Girls' Bits *see also Pregnancy, Sexually Transmitted Diseases, Women*

Girls change during puberty and adolescence, and because girls usually go through this time before boys, you are likely to be moving towards looking like a woman before a boy your age looks like a man. Girls are designed to be perfect for boys . . . God really does know what he's doing!

Vagina (fanny, etc.): This is the passage that you have in the place where boys have a penis. The vagina is designed to let blood out during your monthly periods, and it is also the route out that a baby takes at birth. The vagina entrance has some flabby lips of skin, including the clitoris which makes girls sexually aroused when rubbed. When a girl is getting turned on, the vagina produces a liquid that lubricates and makes it easier for a penis to go in. During sexual intercourse the penis goes into the vagina and moves up and down.

Breasts (tits, boobs, etc.): Breasts are ultimately designed to feed babies after birth, and they grow both during the teenage years and when a woman is pregnant. They can be embarrassing and painful as they develop and during monthly periods. Breasts and nipples are attractive to boys and men.

Give and Take

see also Heartbreak, Lies, Precious

All relationships between people are about give and take, and it's much the same with our relationship with our Creator God. God has given us so much, including our life, the gift of Jesus his Son, and the Holy Spirit to help us. And God wants worship, love, commitment and service from us.

If you've got a boyfriend, you will need to learn to be a giving person and work hard at being unselfish. There will be times when you have to give lots of time and emotional support and help him through tough times. At other times you'll need help and he'll be giving lots of extra support to you. Many boys really take this seriously when they're with a girl. Then there's the reality of giving presents, which lads like.

There may come a time in your relationship when it feels like you're the one who's giving time and energy, and he seems to be doing a lot of taking. All relationships have good and not so good times, but this is a danger sign. Make sure that you can talk about it when you feel this is happening, and be as open as you can about how you feel. If he's not willing to get the balance right and wants everything his way, he may not be the right boy for you.

Gossip

see also Peers, Privacy, Trust

People enjoy talking about other people, and sometimes the things they say are not true. It is possible that you have been the victim of unfair gossip, and so you'll know just how painful it can be.

Both boys and girls love to gossip and can spread rumours about who is going out with who, what they have done and their sexual activity. It's possible for girls who are competing for the attention of the same boys to be really cruel and spread very nasty gossip. Very often gossip is simply lies and it's best not to take it seriously.

Growing

see also Adolescence, Hormones

Adolescence and growing up are a pain! Your body is going through the changes that take you from being a girl to being a woman, but it can be a slow, embarrassing and confusing time.

Growing up means that your limbs will grow so much that they feel like they're not yours, muscles will develop, fat will form where it hasn't been before, breasts will grow, and hair will grow too! You may become smelly and sweaty, your hair may become greasy, and spots could erupt in all the wrong places and at the wrong time. Boys suffer some of these things even more than you do! You'll also find that you're getting taller and wider by the day, and as such you're becoming more attractive to the lads.

Being a teenage girl is not easy, although some girls seem to get through it more quickly and easily than others. And because we're all different, some of your friends will start developing and growing sooner than others. If you look at the heights of a line-up of 14-year-olds, you'll see that some are still very small and others are simply huge!

Hh

Heartbreak *see also Lies, Precious, Rejection*

This sounds really soppy and wet – the thing of silly girls' romance stories! But once you get into a girl-boy relationship, you'll face the risk of heartbreak yourself and you'll probably discover what it really feels like!

Nothing can prepare you for the feeling of joy and happiness and nerves deep inside you when you start to think that you're falling in love with someone. It's like the whole world has become better and brighter, and all you want to do is see him, stare at him and spend time with him . . . great stuff!

But there are no words to describe the feeling of deep sadness and pain when the love you're offering a fit boy isn't returned, or when you've loved and lost him. Those emotional feelings can affect us physically. We can start to feel tired, lose our appetites, get headaches and lose our energy. It can also affect how we see ourselves, and things can become a bit messed up in our minds. But most of all we will feel like someone has got hold of our heart and pulled it apart.

God gave us our emotions, as they help us through life and enhance our senses. But when it hurts, it really does hurt, and it's cruel and selfish either to cause that pain or laugh at others who are going through it. Of course, over time the pain eases and you feel able to start again, looking for the perfect boyfriend. Let's hope you don't get your heart broken too often in the process . . .

Heterosexual *see also Bisexual, Gay, Lesbian*

Most girls and women are 'straight' or heterosexual – they are attracted to the male of the species. This is the way most Christians believe God designed us to be! We are made to want to spend time with the opposite gender, and as we get older we may get to thinking about finding a boy who we really fancy and would consider spending the rest of our life with.

There's a lot of publicity about being homosexual or lesbian – that is, to be attracted to people of the same sex. But most people don't feel those attractions and are quite happy seeking out the opposite.

Holding Hands *see also Activities, Kissing, Petting*

Holding hands is a really nice thing to do and it shows a gentle togetherness as well as feeling really good. Holding hands can be the way you choose to tell your friends that you've become an item and that you're together. This is easier than having to 'announce' it to your group! Lots of people who really care about each other hold hands, and if you care about him, you will too!

Hormones

see also Adolesence, Growing

Hormones are the chemicals inside you that make all the teenage stuff happen, and they really can cause trouble! They go a little mad in teenagers, helping growth and change and making life difficult for those around them. Hormones affect the way you think and behave. They make you interested in boys, but they also help make you moody and irritable and they turn you into a challenging young lady every now and again. Boys suffer more with this, and you've probably noticed their odd and unpredictable actions! Hormones really worry the adults you come into contact with, as they can make you unpredictable and angry for no apparent reason at all!

To cope with some of these hormonal nightmares, you must try to have space to yourself, don't let silly little things get to you, and walk away if you feel yourself getting more and more angry and frustrated. Those hormones are actually doing a good job and this stage will soon pass!

Ii

If You Love Me . . . *see also Love, Petting, Sexual Arousal*

This is a phrase that is often thrown around in one-to-one relationships and it can be a good thing. For instance, if you're feeling neglected or ignored by your boy, you can point it out by challenging his love for you.

But this phrase is much more commonly used when a boy wants to get the girl into sexual activity. He'll have spent time getting to know her and encouraging her to trust him, and then he'll try to go too far in kissing and petting. When she says she's not comfortable about it, he'll use the 'You would if you loved me' line, putting her under pressure to let him do what he wants. This is so wrong and shows that the lad simply sees the girl as someone to be used. There are far too many accounts of girls who have fallen for the line, and as soon as they've slept with the boy they've been dumped.

'If you love me . . .' is no excuse for a boy forcing a girl to do anything. The girl's response has to be 'If you love me you will never put me under any pressure or persuade me to do anything I don't want to do'. That's what real love is about.

Impotence *see also Boys' Bits, Sexual Arousal, Sexual Intercourse*

This is when things are not quite right with a man's bits and he can't get an erection. Some men suffer this when they get older, and it mostly relates to physical problems such as high blood pressure and generally not being fit. Some boys who are getting into sexual activity will find they can't get an erection because they are nervous, worried, shy or feeling guilty about what they're doing.

Incest *see also Paedophiles, Parents, Sexual Abuse*

This is when someone has a sexual relationship with someone they are closely related to. It has been known for brothers and sisters, separated and brought up in different families, to meet and fall in love when they are older. But incest is often in the home and generally relates to abuse of children by a parent or older brother or sister. There are no reasons or excuses for older young people or adults developing a sexual relationship with a younger person in the family – this is always wrong.

Men who abuse girls, particularly their own daughters or young sisters, use the excuse that it's their job to initiate their daughter gently into sexual activity. This is total rubbish! If something like this has happened to you, it is really important that you talk to someone whom you respect and who understands you, and you need to remember that you are not responsible for what happened.

Internet Dangers *see also Chat Rooms, Cyber Sex, Internet Sites, Paedophiles*

The internet has a huge amount of bad, dangerous and simply wrong stuff on it! There are sites full of pornography and other images that encourage people to abuse and hurt others, and there are chat rooms where adults who want to cause young people harm pretend to be young in order to develop relationships. These paedophiles will try to get personal information, and will use it to trace girls and make contact by meeting up, pretending to be young. They're often very clever in the way they do this, but they are generally motivated by a desire to sexually abuse young ladies like you, so you must be careful!

If you use the internet (and you'd be a bit of an exception if you didn't!), stick to sites and services which are suited to your age, tell your parents or other adults what you're doing, and don't keep things secret. Then you'll keep yourself safe and you'll have nothing to worry about.

Internet Sites *see also Chat Rooms, Cyber Sex, Internet Dangers*

There's a lot of information out there and it doesn't take long to find websites that will help you with relationships and offer advice on sex. There are some set up by the BBC, youth agencies, church groups and health agencies which can help you, and they're easy to find. But, like all other advice, they all have a particular angle, and their information has a message they want to get over which may be different from what Christians would say. Many local authority, health authority and government information sites are concerned about teenage pregnancy and sexual health, so their focus will be on having safe sex by using condoms or other contraception, not about the right time and age to begin engaging in sexual activity.

Internet sites can be set up by anyone, so you should be very careful about trusting all the information you read, and instead talk about it with leaders and friends who have experience.

Jj

Jealousy *see also Appearance, Lies, Peers, Self-Worth*

If you're going out with the best-looking fit lad around, there are going to be other girls who are jealous of you, and there may be lads who are jealous of him too! But how would you feel if another girl moved in on your object of desire? You'd probably feel a bit jealous!

Jealousy is something that we all suffer from and we all need to be really wary of. Jealousy is like a rot that can eat away and make people more and more bitter, and that bitterness leads to irrational actions and attitudes that in the cold light of day, when you've calmed down and thought it through, just don't make any sense at all! Jealousy between friends over a boy is really common and can damage your friendships for life.

God's got a plan for you, and although it may not be what you think you want right now, it will be ideal, perfect and wonderful. So there's no point being jealous of others, because you've got good stuff to come.

Kk

Kissing

see also Boyfriends, Love, Sexual Arousal

Kissing is an expression of love and tenderness, although I guess not all the people you've kissed are people you fancy! There's something really gross about having to kiss that ancient uncle who always insists on a peck on the cheek, and a quick snog behind the shed in the garden with the boy next door when you were both 7 doesn't really count either!

Lots of people will offer you advice about kissing and some may be useful. But if you and your lad are getting into kissing, he won't like the idea of you having discussed your every move with your mates! Kissing is special, but it's only special when it's meant to be special – when two people are showing their affection for each other in a loving way.

Of course, there are some basics about kissing. You need to make sure your mouth is clear of all food, your breath doesn't smell rotten and you've cleaned your teeth. If you get into tongues in each other's mouth, remember that this is actually quite intimate and personal, and boys will probably want to force this more than girls. Kissing can also cause you to get sexually excited, and so it is best to learn to control yourself and behave properly.

Ll

Law

see also Abstinence, Incest, Sexual Abuse

Nearly all countries in the world have laws about sex and relationships. Most say that incest is wrong, and some have very strong penalties for family members who have sexual relationships with each other. All countries say that sexual abuse by an adult on a child is wrong and have criminal penalties. Many countries have minimum ages for sexual activities between young people who have both willingly given their permission, with some countries choosing different ages for same-sex activity.

In most of the UK, 16 has been set as the acceptable age for young people to take part in sexual activity, but older adults could be committing an offence if they are in positions of responsibility (teachers, youth leaders, etc.) and have persuaded the young person to take part. However, it is unlikely that a young sexually active couple over 13 will be prosecuted. In the rest of Europe the ages vary, with 12 being the lowest age. In the United States the age of consent is set by each state, and this can sometimes vary between girls and boys. Most choose an age between 16 and 18. Some counties within USA states also have laws about teenagers and sexual activity.

The law is only part of the story. Just because the law says it is not illegal to have sex aged 16, that doesn't make it right for you or make you ready to get involved that young. Everyone develops at a different rate, and despite the fact that most 16-year-old girls are more physically and emotionally developed than most boys of the same age, that still doesn't mean girls are ready for sex. The most important thing is that God made sex to be a really special thing, and to be kept for a really special time between a man and woman who want to be together for life. You can waste this really special experience if you jump into bed too soon, particularly if the boy you are with is not as keen as you are . . . and you'll set a really rubbish example of God's love at the same time. Any girl who is forced into sexual activity has a right to report the boy, and in extreme cases this could be classed as rape. Of course, God forgives, but he wants the very best for you, so don't rush it!

Lesbian *see also Bisexual, Crush, Gay, Heterosexual*

A lesbian girl is one who is attracted to other girls in the same way as a gay boy is drawn to other boys. Some experts say that one in every ten women is actually lesbian, although not all of those are in lesbian relationships. Some of your friends may be wondering if they are lesbian and may be feeling attracted to you or to other girls. They may be confused by those feelings and may be suffering guilt and worry too.

It is normal for some girls to be attracted to other girls, particularly older ones, while they go through puberty and move towards being women. The same happens with boys. Some adolescent girls look up to other girls or women as role models and even feel that they fancy them. In most cases this soon passes and is replaced by a deep desire to get to know boys. Because many young people are getting into sexual activity at a younger age, it's possible that a girl will think that she is lesbian and decide on it too soon, when really she is only going through a time of discovery. Some girls will become sexually active with both boys and girls, often described as bisexual. But for a few the feelings linger and the attraction to other females grows stronger. It is often tough for people who feel they are gay, and many struggle with those feelings and try to keep them hidden.

As with studies into men, there are lots of theories as to why this happens for around 10 per cent of girls, but no one really knows. It's also similar with what happens when boys grow up, in that some boys go through a phase of fancying other lads before settling on women instead!

Girls face a really tough time as they get older and as some of those around them boast (honestly or not!) of getting into relationships and sex. If they get too well known for getting through boyfriends, they will be seen and described by boys as tarts and described really negatively, and if they choose to avoid lads for a while or not get into too heavy stuff, they'll be accused of being lesbian. This is really bad – it is unpleasant and does not show respect.

Lies

see also Ending, Give and Take, Privacy, Trust

There are a lot of things that can damage relationships, and one of the most important is a lack of truth! Lies and dishonesty are all around when it comes to relationships and sex, so be careful not to be dragged in!

Many young people lie about what they do, when they do it and who they do it with! There are regular surveys of the sexual activity of young people, but the problem is that anyone can lie in a survey! It's generally thought that boys boast and lie more about this than girls. Your friends may boast of things they have done, films they have watched or substances they've taken (always a stupid thing to do!) but the chances are that these are lies – the product of their vivid imaginations! It's easy to fall for these lies and believe that every other girl has a sexy boyfriend, or that if you're not snogging, you're weird – but that's simply not true!

People lie about others in order to make them seem worse than they really are. Girls are sometimes the victims of these lies, rumours and gossip. Try to remember that God made us all and he loves us all so much that he hates to see people hurting each other or causing any pain. If you go along with the lies about others, you are contributing to the hurt that is being caused.

If you've got a boyfriend, it's really important that you are honest with him – but do it gently! If you feel it's time to move on out of the relationship, make it clear and don't keep him hanging on. And it's really cruel to play around with his feelings by messing around with other boys at the same time. Try to think how you would like to be treated and treat him the same way.

God knows what is right and true, and that's why he made us as we are and set standards for us to live by. The world lies to us all about love, romance and relationships, and makes out that things will always be better and easier than they really are. Get real, stick to the truth and ignore the lies and the liars!

Lifelong Partner

see also Boyfriends, Marriage

Something really special may happen to you soon . . . or in some years' time! It's weird to think that quite a lot of married couples met and first started going out with each other as teenagers and have managed to keep their relationship strong. Some girls have a number of boyfriends before they find someone who they really love and want to spend the rest of their lives with. Others decide that marriage and long-term commitments are not for them and choose not to follow that path.

God's got a plan for you, even though you don't know what it is! Part of that plan could be that you say 'yes' to the next lad who asks you out, and once he's your boyfriend you both enjoy the relationship so much that you decide you simply want to stay together. But it's much more likely that your boyfriends will be great but not ever-lasting, and it could be some way down the line before your future husband appears on the scene. But don't worry, don't rush and don't panic – God knows what he's doing!

Love

see also Desire, Heartbreak, Precious

What is love? It is not an act or an activity. It is not a word to use freely or something that you make. It is not easy, cheap, lust or sex. Love is much more personal, deep and powerful than all that.

You will have experienced the warmth and familiarity of love from your parents or other adults who have cared for you. Love can be the really strong bond you feel for a close friend who has been good to you and whom you want to help. Ruth and Naomi in the Bible had a really close, loving friendship. Love is something that God is always giving us through the good things we have and the constant forgiveness for when we get it wrong. Love is Jesus dying on the cross and saying, 'I did it for you. Now all you have to do is love me.'

Love in a relationship can really seem like the real thing. Love is what happens when you think you've met the guy of your dreams. Love makes you think about him all the time, it makes your insides churn like a cement mixer when you see him, and it makes you want to do things you've never done before . . . like going to car rallies! Love may even cause you to enjoy his jokes! Love is patient, kind, polite, good, true and eternal. God made us to want love and to give love in order to make our lives even better, so it is a good, natural and right emotion to feel.

Love is about giving and receiving, and it's about the great feeling that you can trust someone else fully and completely and that neither of you is holding anything back. Real love is something you will only know when you experience it and it's impossible to put into words!

Unfortunately, these feelings, which we all experience, are not always about real love. We may think we love someone when really we just fancy them or have a bit of a crush on them. If you get it wrong and the person you think you love doesn't love you, it can be really painful and may put you off 'love' for a while. But once the next object of desire comes along, the feelings will start again and, sooner or later, the true love of your life, who you'll settle down with, will set your heart on fire.

Mm

Magazines

see also Advice, Pornography

Teenage magazines are usually aimed at girls and you're probably familiar with them. Many have good things to offer and some very dodgy things too. They are often dominated by articles, photo features and problem pages about relationships and sex. They show images of beauty and body profiles that are not realistic. They don't always give the sort of advice that is either helpful or right. They encourage young people like you to get into relationships before you may want to or before you've found a boy you really like. They can give the impression that every other teenager is in a relationship and that many are having a great time getting into sexual activity. This is not true and not helpful! If you do look at these magazines, read them with caution and think, 'What does God think about this?'

Make-Up

see also Appearance

There's lots of make-up available and plenty of top tips for looking good, playing down your worst features and accentuating your best ones! Magazines, books, beauty therapists and TV programmes are full of ways to use make-up to look good. There's nothing wrong with using make-up as long as you keep in under control and don't let it take over! There's nothing less attractive to the average boy than a girl whose make-up cracks when she smiles because it has been put on too thick!

Make-up is about image and you really need to think about how you want to look. Remember that God made you as you are and many lads go for the natural look. And on the practical side make-up costs lots of cash and takes ages to put on and clean off!

Marriage

see also Adultery, Divorce, Love

God rates marriage. He invented it so that both man and woman can feel secure and be able to trust each other. The vows made during the wedding service are commitments for life, not just until it gets too hard to bother to try or until someone else comes along. Marriage is God's ideal situation for children to grow up secure and happy. Marriage takes work, a sense of humour, heaps of forgiveness and lots of patience.

Marriages do go wrong, and some people suggest that it is better to live together instead of getting married. But marriage is special, and being married can help people hold on to their love and have a really happy life by working at it, rather than simply giving up at the first problem and walking away.

Marriage should be for life, so it's something that should be gone into only when you're really sure. You need time to enjoy yourself as an individual first before tying yourself to someone else. And marriage is no answer to problems, so don't think of it as the easy option. But good marriages can be great, exciting, comforting and really good to see as well as experience.

Marriage is, according to the Bible, where sex should take place. Because sexual activity is private and personal, it can only be really good in a relationship that means a lot to both people. In marriage the man and woman have made a lifelong commitment to each other and want the best for the other, so sex can be total and complete, without fear of being used or abused. In a marriage a girl can give herself fully and completely without fear. Sex before marriage is common but not as good as sex in marriage – and not the way God made it.

Masturbation

see also Abstinence, Gay, Lesbian, Love, Self-Worth, Sexual Arousal

Many girls masturbate. They sometimes stimulate themselves by touch or using something to rub themselves. This is a natural part of growing up and self-discovery. Most boys also masturbate by playing with their penis.

Some Christians have concerns about masturbation. It is a private and personal thing to do, yet relationships are not personal and private in that way and it would be better to spend time building up friendships. Many people don't want to think about the fact that girls do this. Masturbation can become habit-forming and therefore almost an addiction.

When you do it you may think of boys or men and fantasise about them or look at pornographic magazines with 'sexy' pictures of naked men. Yet God didn't make anyone – male or female – to be objects thought of and used in that way.

You are not doing anything that other girls aren't doing and so you shouldn't worry that you are in some way weird. But do think about the downside too and talk to an adult you trust to find out their point of view. And don't forget that you can be honest with Jesus about anything, including this.

Men

see also Equality, Growing, Independence, Women

The boys all around you at school or in church will soon be men! This may be exciting for some and very scary for others! Men have all the things that girls find attractive. They have muscles, a shape that appeals to women, and a bum and other bits that girls like.

Men have traditionally been expected to be strong and to keep their emotions to themselves. In the past they were the ones who went to work and earned money to keep the family, while most married women stayed at home and looked after the children.

Manhood is changing. Men are not always the main wage earners in many households, and some stay at home to look after the house and children while the woman goes to work. Men can no longer be guaranteed work in traditional industries, and many older men find it hard to accept that things are changing. Men are growing up in a new world with new attitudes about what men and women should be like. Men are now more able to share the work of looking after babies, to show their feelings, and to be sensitive and kind instead of hard and macho. Men will still generally want to show care and protection to their girlfriend or wife, and there's nothing wrong with that. A man does not have the right to abuse the woman he is in a relationship with, even if in the past that may have happened. God values men and women equally and can use us just the same.

Miscarriage

see also Precious, Pregnancy

This is when a baby is born far too soon to be able to survive, often in the first three months of a pregnancy but potentially at any time during pregnancy. It may seem to the mother that they are bleeding, as during a period, but the unformed baby is part of the blood. Sometimes miscarriages are caused by the health of the mother carrying the baby, the stress they are going through and also their age, but in most cases there is no explanation . . . it just happens in nearly one in every four pregnancies. The birth of a dead child after 24 weeks of pregnancy, which often looks like a fully formed baby, is called a stillbirth.

A miscarriage or stillbirth is a really sad thing to happen to anyone and can have long and deep consequences for the girl or woman involved. They will have started the emotional attachment with the unborn foetus, and it is very difficult for many to come to terms with the death of that little unformed and developing child.

If this happens to someone who is close to you, they will need a great deal of help and support to get through it. You'll need to be there for them, allow them to cry and talk, and understand a little of the pain that they're going through.

Oo

One-Night Stand

see also Promiscuous, Sexually Transmitted Diseases

Some boys, men, women and girls boast about having 'one-night stands' and pretend that they really enjoy them. A one-night stand is simply a very short-term sexual relationship that is over by the following morning. For example, a woman may go out to a club and try to 'pick up' a lad, the aim being to end up in bed with him. Once the sexual act is over, so is the relationship . . . even if that's not what the boy wants.

There is a huge number of problems with this way of behaving. One-night stands are one of the main ways to become infected with a sexually transmitted disease (STD) and puts both partners at great risk of painful and potentially serious illness. One-night stands are often motivated by a lustful desire that has nothing to do with God's plan for sex. We're not made to 'use' other people for our own satisfaction, and to do so is wrong. One-night stands can become a really bad habit, where a man or woman becomes obsessed with sleeping around and takes more and more risks in order to get the 'high' that they desire. But, most of all, one-night stands are empty and meaningless, often leading to self-loathing, loneliness and deep hurt. Many people who have behaved like this when younger find it really tough to get into good, healthy relationships with others, and find it hard to trust others for the long haul.

TV and films are sometimes guilty of promoting a 'laddish' culture of going out, getting drunk, sleeping around and having 'fun'. This isn't really fun at all – it's a sad and empty way to live.

Oral Sex

see also Sexual Activity, Sexual Arousal, Sexual Intercourse, Sexually Transmitted Diseases

In simple terms this is sexual activity that has something to do with the mouth. You may have read about it in magazines or heard it mentioned in sex education at school.

When in a deep, long-term and very personal relationship with someone, it is really enjoyable to explore each other's bodies in many different ways. One of the ways is to kiss, lick or suck parts of the body, including the sexual organs. The obvious risks include the stimulation this can cause, which almost inevitably leads to full sexual intercourse, and the exchange of bodily fluids which can lead to contracting diseases. Girls are sometimes forced into this before they are ready or when they really don't want to. It is always wrong to be forced in that way, and if someone tries to force you, you must say 'no'.

Oral sex is not an alternative to 'full' sex and not any less serious or important. Because it involves so much personal contact, like sexual intercourse it should be kept within lifelong commitments.

Pp

Paedophiles *see also Pornography, Sexual Abuse*

There's always a lot of media attention when a child goes missing and often paedophiles are thought to be responsible. A paedophile is someone who is sexually attracted to children and they will often want to put that attraction into practice by engaging in various forms of sexual activity with young people. This is always sexual abuse and is always wrong.

Paedophiles are not usually the 'dirty old men' that newspapers like to show us. Most abuse is committed by men (and sometimes women) against children or teenagers, and many of those involved are either family members, close friends or people in positions of trust such as priests, vicars, teachers, youth leaders and so on. This obviously doesn't mean that all those who work with children and young people are attracted to them, but it does mean that schools, churches, clubs and youth organisations have to be very careful to make sure that people working with them are checked out.

No one really knows why people are sexually attracted to children, but there are lots of theories and ideas. We can be sure that God loves children and Jesus spoke of harsh punishments for anyone who harms them. If you've come into contact with a paedophile, you might need to talk it through with someone and pray that God will help you and also help that person who has gone so wrong and caused so much harm.

Parents *see also Adolescence, Advice, Men, Women*

They're not from another planet . . . although at times it might seem as if they are! You may often have prayed, asking God why he gave you the parents you've got instead of the parents of your friends! God chose you for them and them for you, strange as it seems! Parents are important to all of us, even if we don't live with both of them, and in nearly all cases parents really care about you and want the very best for you.

Parents are going to be really nervous about you getting into relationships. They may be really open about sex and what happens to your body as you go through puberty, or they may have been a bit shy about it and left it to school to tell you about it. They will be concerned that you don't get hurt by falling too far in love with the first boy who shows a bit of interest in you, and they'll feel your pain if it all goes wrong. They'll naturally be worried that you won't be able to say 'no' and you'll lose your virginity and end up getting into stuff that you're really not ready for. Dads are usually particularly concerned about their daughters and will want to protect them, even if it seems like they've not noticed that you've grown up! Many parents of boys are scared that their son will end up making a girl pregnant and have to grow up really quickly and face the consequences of this seriously adult situation.

Your parents may be really confused about all this going on and they may struggle with being parents of a teenager. They'll wonder what happened to their lovely, pretty and gentle little girl! There are going to be arguments, rows, confusion and stresses, but in the end they really do love you. And because they love you, there'll be times when they say 'no' and when they set boundaries and rules which make you really angry! It's tough when it happens, but they're probably only trying to help you in the long term. And it's worth remembering that, just like you, parents make mistakes too and are simply trying to do their best.

The best way to get through all of this is to communicate with them. Do all you can to keep them on your side, show them affection and tell them how you're feeling. Be as open as you can and don't keep secrets or personal feelings too hidden away. You may well find that when you've been chucked by a boy or you don't know how to attract the one you like the look of, your parents may be able to help. Ancient as they are, they were young once and went through it too!

Peers

see also Abstinence, Advice, Precious

If you look at all the girls your age, you'll see a great difference between them. Some will be well into growing up, while others will seem to be much younger in their size and the way they look. It is good to hang out with girls the same age as you are and they can be a great help to you. You should be able to chat things over with them and even compare yourself to how they are doing and feel good about it! But you need to be wise about it too, because not all of your girl friends will be a good influence on you.

One of the main reasons why girls get into relationships too quickly is because of peer pressure either from their own girl friends or from boys. Many of your friends may be getting boyfriends (or may say they have them) and they may suggest that you're weird because you don't have a boyfriend. They may boast about kissing, touching or sexual activity with their lad, even though it is often not true. Some boys still think that they're big men if they have lots of girlfriends, and girls will pretend they're grown up by letting boys mess with them, but really they are wasting the great gift of love. Friends may tease you because you're not into boys, but if they loosen up too much and have too many relationships they'll be accused of being cheap and 'easy'.

This peer pressure can be really strong and it is hard to be different. But if we think of the greatest people in the Bible, they were all people who didn't go along with the crowd and did their own thing instead. It takes a stronger woman to stick to her beliefs than to go along with what everyone else does!

Penis

see Boys' Bits

Perfection

see also Appearance, Attraction, Lies, Precious, Self-Worth

There is no one who is perfect in every way and, sadly, as a teenage girl you're not even going to be close to perfect! There will be others who look at you and see the spots or the brace on your teeth, the greasy hair, the developing breasts or the regular blushes! You should always try to make a difference to yourself by being clean, but that won't change the things that are going on as you grow and develop.

Magazines and TV show us images of perfection which you're never going to reach, and once someone falls in love with you, you'll realise that it doesn't matter if you look like a model or not! In the same way, you may have an idea in your head of what a perfect guy is like, but once you meet the one God has got for you, you'll forget those false ideas of perfection and be really happy with the one who is perfect for you!

There are some who spend their whole lives waiting for the perfect love that never comes along, and that's such a waste! God wants us to be happy in our own skins, and he should know because he made us as we are!

Periods

see also Girls' Bits, PMS, Women

Boys should all be really relieved that they don't suffer from periods, a natural and necessary part of the life of every girl! Most girls start their periods when they reach puberty and their body is changing, which can be any time between 8 and 17. Each month their body prepares to become pregnant by releasing an egg and making the lining of the womb thicker in order to cushion the egg if it is fertilised. When the time to become pregnant each month passes and the egg is not fertilised by a boy's sperm, the extra lining comes away and exits the girl's body in the form of blood. Girls and women usually wear pads or tampons to soak up the blood during their periods.

You may already know that the monthly period can be very frightening, particularly at first, and should never be laughed about. It's often accompanied by stomach pains and aches, and occasionally by headaches and sickness. Many girls and women can become moody leading up to the time each month because the chemicals in their bodies are changing.

Many men joke about how they suffer when their wife or girlfriend is going through their period, but it really is no fun. When the time comes around each month for your period, you will need plenty of care, consideration and understanding, so tell your boy that you need extra care. If your period is a few days late, it may mean that you're a little tired and rundown or may have a minor illness. A late period can also be a sign of pregnancy. Whatever the reason, it's worth getting it checked out.

Petting

see also Foreplay, Pregnancy

This seems like an old-fashioned word or something to do with looking after pets! Petting in girl-boy relationships is what happens when you want to get to know each other better physically. Petting can be fun . . . and it can also be really, really risky!

When you get into petting, you'll probably start with kissing, and that kissing will become more intense and exciting. At the same time you may want to stroke the hair of your boyfriend, cuddle or touch his body in other places. His reaction is likely to be to want to do the same to you. This is all part of exploration and discovering other people, but it can be sexually arousing too. When you get really excited sexually, then it can become quite difficult to stop and get yourself in control again, and petting becomes foreplay with the natural conclusion of sexual intercourse. Boys find it even more difficult to stop once they're excited and their penis is erect. It begins to get really risky if either of you starts to remove clothes – this is a danger sign.

Christians have a range of views about petting. Some would say that any form of intimate touching and passionate kissing is wrong because of the difficulty in stopping if you get too worked up. Others take the view that it's one of those things that young people do, and they should do it but know the limits and not go into full sexual intercourse . . . but that's not easy!

So let's be honest – you're probably going to want to get to know your boyfriend by petting, and if your relationship is growing, he may be keen for some physical contact beyond holding hands too. If so, you need to make sure that you are both ready for touching and both decide at the outset what is off-limits. You should never be forced to do anything you don't want to, and you should never do anything you feel is wrong – listen to your conscience! Most importantly for girls: keep your clothes on!

Physical Abuse

see also Self-Worth, Sexual Abuse, Suicide

Physical abuse is not about sexual abuse and paedophiles. Physical abuse is about someone being injured by hitting, burning, slapping, beating and so on. Physical abuse is all about power – the abuser wants to have power and control over the other and often feels really frustrated that they have no power in any other way. This is not a good situation and anyone physically injured by someone else should not have to put up with it.

You may have been the victim of someone physically abusing you, and this could make you more wary about touching people or others touching you. Some boys and men enjoy having physical power over girls and beat them. Domestic abuse is a problem in some marriages and relationships and is usually (but not always) inflicted on women by men. Often people who have witnessed or been victims of physical abuse find it more difficult to trust others, so if you've been through things in the past, you may need your boy to be really gentle and understanding. Be open about your experiences and learn to trust again.

PMS

see also Girls' Bits, Periods, Women

This stands for Pre-Menstrual Stress, sometimes known as PMT (Pre-Menstrual Tension). It is thought that about 90 per cent of all girls and women who have periods go through some days of this before their period. This is probably due to changes in the hormones in your body, but it isn't clear why some girls suffer more than others.

If you suffer from PMS, you will already know some of the many symptoms of it. These include being irritable and moody, losing confidence in yourself, being aggressive, tiredness, poor concentration. You may also have tender breasts, headaches, weight gain and swollen ankles.

If you have a boyfriend, he may find it really tough to understand what you are going through, and you could be suffering so much that you find it difficult to explain to him. Try to be aware of what's happening to you and tell him if you can.

You can ease some of the symptoms of PMS by trying to keep fit and do gentle exercise, changing to a healthier diet and not smoking. There are medicines and vitamin supplements if it gets really bad, but seek medical help and advice before taking anything.

Pornography

see also Certificate 18, Law, Men, Precious

Porn is pictures, photographs, videos, magazines and books that contain sexual content and are designed to cause sexual excitement. To be honest, it's not easy to avoid pornography, which at its least harmful is topless girls in daily newspapers. Porn is very easily available in shops and on the internet, which is full of 18+ websites with very inappropriate images and videos. The problem in our modern world is that pornography is very easily accessible and is seen as perfectly acceptable and good fun.

You may have known boys who've looked at a magazine of naked women and had a laugh about it, but pornography is wrong and really rubbish stuff for many reasons. Pictures of naked women or men in sexual poses cheapens what God designed love to be and turns something beautiful into something tacky and sleazy. People whose images appear in porn are being used, whether they agree to do what they're doing or not. Porn gives us a distorted and weird view of the value of other people, who should never be viewed as objects to be stared at and lusted after. Porn suggests that everyone is into things that in many cases are pretty nasty, and there's never any mention of the risks of sexually transmitted diseases or abuse. Easy access to porn feeds the desires of paedophiles who want to abuse children and young people. Porn makes money at the expense of people whose lives are damaged by it. Need I go on?! Keep your thoughts focused on God's moral code, which talks about keeping ourselves, including our thoughts, pure, and avoid this bad stuff.

Precious

see also Appearance, Self-Worth

Lives are precious, people's feelings are precious, and love is precious! Everything about relationships is precious and special, and you need to keep that in your mind!

God wants us to treat other people as we would like to be treated and never do anything that causes pain and harm. Once you've got a boyfriend, you will have a very special feeling of concern and love for him, and this is a really precious thing. He is willing to trust you, to walk with you through the tough times of being a teenage girl, and to give you support. He will trust you with his feelings and secrets, which is not easy for a boy to do. He may be more open with you than he's ever been with anyone else. He is giving you a precious opportunity to learn about boys.

The precious, special feelings in a relationship can easily be wrecked by lies, deception, two-timing, betraying trust, and forcing things. If your lad doesn't treat you as precious, you may need to think about whether you should be together. If you remember that you're both precious, you'll succeed in your relationship and learn what love is about.

Pregnancy

see also Contraception, Sexual Intercourse, Sexually Transmitted Diseases, Termination

When a girl becomes pregnant, she has the very beginnings of another human life inside her, and even though it is probably not able to survive outside her womb until around 24 weeks, it is still a life. Pregnancy is a really, really special thing, designed by God to help us populate the world and to enjoy as part of a lifelong commitment to each other and to the unborn child.

There are many myths around about how girls become pregnant and you'll have heard them! Girls can't become pregnant on their own – there has to be a boy involved! The egg in the girl's womb has to be fertilised by one of the millions of sperm that a boy produces when he ejaculates. Having sex standing up doesn't stop pregnancy. Usually the sperm reaches the egg by full sexual intercourse, but it is possible to get pregnant from sperm on the boy's fingers or penis before he ejaculates.

The consequences of pregnancy are either wonderful or dire, depending on your situation. For a settled, married couple there'll be lots of excitement and joy about a pregnancy, but for two young people who were having a bit of fun that went too far there'll be heaps of fear, shame, damage and wrecked relationships. Lives can change dramatically, with plans going down the drain and both future parents having to grow up really quickly and make decisions and take responsibility that they're not ready for. The only way to be 100 per cent sure of not getting pregnant is not to have sexual intercourse with a boy or man, and avoid any situations where you both end up in private and are tempted to go too far. The cost is simply too great.

Privacy

see also Activities, Lies, Trust

There are times when you need to be private, and times when you need the things you say and do to be kept private. As you grow up, you'll want to have time and space to yourself without your parents, brothers or sisters in your space. Your bedroom may be your private space or you may have somewhere else you go. The important thing is that you get that time alone and allow others to have their private time and space too.

You'll probably have more need for privacy than your boyfriend. When you're in a relationship, you'll want to be with him all the time at the beginning, but as your relationship grows, you may start to feel a bit trapped. This is often because you've not had any space and may be feeling all your time is eaten up by your boyfriend. It can work the other way too, with him really needing a break from you but you not seeing the signs! The best way to cope with all this is to be open and honest all the way through and trust enough to give each other some space.

You and your boyfriend will need time together and some of that time will need to be in private. Of course, when you get into kissing and petting, there are risks which you must be aware of, so you'll need to be careful about just how private you are. But you will need time together to talk, help each other through tough times, and share fun and laughter.

In relationships you'll get to know private things about your boyfriend, and some girls use that info badly when the relationship ends by spreading gossip and abusing the trust the lad put in her. Imagine for a minute how you would feel if something you'd told your boy in private that you'd never told anyone else was passed around as gossip and everyone seemed to know? Even if you split up badly and there's lots of hurt and pain around, that's no excuse for betraying someone's trust by making something private into public knowledge. Privacy and trust are important to us all, and if it is broken, it can take ages to mend.

Promiscuous *see also Precious, Self-Worth, Trust*

There are people who are promiscuous, which means they sleep around a lot and have had lots of sexual partners, sometimes on one-night stands. This is so far from what God wanted when he made us, and there's quite a lot in the Bible about people who have no respect for their own bodies or the lives of others. God didn't design us to use people by sleeping with them and then discarding them, and anyone who does that is sinning big-time! Girls (and boys) who are promiscuous also get a bad name for themselves and prove that they can't be trusted. And all that's before we consider the risks of diseases!

Sleeping around is not something to be encouraged or be proud of. Don't believe the lies of those who claim to be having lots of sex with different people, and don't envy them . . . they're just wrong!

Qq

Queer

see also Gay, Lesbian

This is a way people describe homosexuals. Most people find it an offensive and insulting term.

Rr

Rape

see also Law, Sexual Abuse, Sexual Arousal

Rape is violent sexual assault, which often includes sexual intercourse but can also include oral sex and male gay sexual acts. The key thing about rape is that the person being raped has not given permission for the sexual act to take place and is being forced to do it. That 'forcing' can include coercion and persuasion as well as physical force. Date rape often takes place when two people have got together, kissed and so on, and one of the two has decided to take things further without the other one being willing. Occasionally there is evidence of drugs or strong alcohol being added to the victim's drinks to make them sleepy or less aware of what's going on. Rape is not only about boys and men attacking girls and women – there are women who rape men, women who rape other women, and men who rape men.

Rape is violent, abusive, illegal, dangerous and very damaging. The use of other people as sexual objects is entirely wrong and against God's will for us, and no one has the right to force anyone to do anything they don't want to do. Our bodies are very precious and personal to us, and when they are violated by rape, some people find it very difficult to get over that abuse.

It is thought that there are more instances of rape than are ever reported, but, on the other hand, there have been cases of people saying they have been raped when they consented to the act but got 'cold feet' and were full of regret afterwards. A false accusation of rape can also destroy lives.

Many boys are tempted to go further with girls than they know they should, and once they get sexually excited, they may find they can't stop, whatever the girl may be saying or asking. In a situation like that, the boy could find himself accused of rape. You may be the victim of a boy wanting to go too far, and you need to be firm and make sure he clearly gets the 'no' message. God wants us to keep ourselves pure, respect other people and their bodies, and keep sex for that special relationship.

Rebellion

see also Adolescence, Hormones, Parents

So who do you know who is perfect? Who do you know who has never rebelled and wanted to do the opposite of what was asked of them? It's worth asking your parents about their teenage years and their times of rebellion. If they say they never rebelled about anything, they're probably not telling the truth! Your dad may have some really dramatic stories because boys often rebel more than girls. Most of the main Bible characters we read about and look up to rebelled at some time or another. David rebelled when power went to his head and he desired another man's wife. Moses rebelled when he got angry with God and argued back. Peter rebelled when he claimed three times that he had nothing to do with Jesus! The common thread in those stories is that God understood them and forgave them when they turned back to him.

It's part of growing up to go through times when you want to rebel against what your parents, your church or even your friends stand for. You won't want to follow rules and regulations at home or at school, you'll want to run away from the pressures of exams and escape the 'normal' way of doing things, and you'll want to ignore the advice of anyone who suggests you may not be getting everything right!

Of course, you may rebel when it comes to boyfriends. You may want to stay out later than you're told to, be more sexually active than you know would be approved of, or go out with a lad you know your parents will not think is a good choice! Your parents may not approve of your boy for lots of good reasons, but you stay with him in order to prove something to them. The problem with this is that you'll end up hurting and using many people (including yourself) if you follow that path. Many girls who have done that realise their mistakes some years afterwards with real and deep regret.

If you've grown up in church, you may find that you want to rebel against Christian teaching and lifestyle, and you may want to go really wild in order to prove something . . . but you're not quite sure what! It is really important that you come to a personal faith in God and not just go along with it because you always have, and that you ask the Holy

Spirit to give you the strength to live as God wants. The funny thing about all this is that Christians are the real rebels – they have chosen not to live the easy, weak and harmful way of the world, but to live differently as God planned. That is really rebellious!

Rejection

see also Dumping, Heartbreak, Lies, Self-Worth

It is so difficult and so painful to feel rejected, and yet it is something we all have to go through.

You may already know what it feels like to be rejected by a boy you really want to go out with. You'll have felt as if your whole world has fallen apart, and you'll wonder if you'll ever get over the pain that weighs you down. You may also doubt that the embarrassment will ever lift, and you'll be afraid to go out because, for some strange reason, you think the whole world knows that you've been turned down!

Rejection goes right to the depths of how you see yourself. If you don't rate yourself anyway and you're always looking in the mirror and wishing you were different, rejection will come as no surprise but will only serve to confirm that you are useless. If you're used to success, rejection will be a whole new, and not pleasant, experience.

You are of value, you are different from anyone else, and God made you as you are because that's how he wanted you to be. That might seem difficult to believe, but if you don't accept it, you're saying that God got it wrong!

If someone rejects you, it's their loss, not yours. Rejection doesn't happen often and can be survived. Rejection can remind us that we're not attractive to everyone, even if your dad tells you you're the most beautiful girl ever! If you go through rejection, pick yourself up, dust yourself off and thrust yourself into the world again!

Respect

see also Appearance, Attraction, Lies, Perfection, Precious, Self-Worth

God made us all and he loves us all. He is upset and hurt when we choose to cause pain to others, but he forgives us and helps us through. We can avoid causing pain and hurt by respecting those around us and particularly by showing respect for friends and boyfriends.

If you respect someone, you will want to know what they think about things and you'll want to spend time listening to their views. You'll enjoy being in their company and so you'll do nothing that will badly affect your great relationship. You'll want to put their needs first and do all you can to show them that you rate them.

Respect is often discussed in sex ed and relationship counselling. Boys, who are often physically stronger, can sometimes put girls under pressure to kiss, cuddle or take part in sexual acts that the girl doesn't really want to. If your boy respects you, he'll never do that.

You may struggle with self-respect too. If you feel that you're not as good, good-looking, glamorous, sexy or bright as other girls, you may think you're worthless. You may also get into stuff that's harmful such as smoking, drugs or sex because you simply don't care about yourself. If you need to boost your self-respect, get help from your girl friends and older people who you think will understand. And remember that God respects you, wants you to respect others and wants you to learn to really respect and value yourself.

Ss

Self-Worth

see Appearance, Attraction, Lies, Precious, Respect

I doubt if any girl or boy has ever gone through adolescence and been happy with themselves all the way through – it is just not possible!

Lots of your friends and peers will appear to be confident and happy with themselves, but underneath they'll be just as confused as you are! Many girls struggle with their own self-image, wishing they were more attractive or more grown-up. Like you, they'll look in the mirror and not like what they see because it doesn't match up to the images we are sold by the media. But even in this confused state you may be attractive to lads, and that could boost your confidence a bit. Even if that's not happening for you, God still thinks you're great!

At this stage of your life you are going through a time of great change, and the 'you' that you see now will have changed massively in four or five years' time. You will look different and have much more confidence. You will have developed new skills, you may have found success in love, developed friendships that will last and got in with a group of peers who are supportive and helpful.

Sexual Abuse

see also Incest, Paedophiles, Physical Abuse, Pornography

Sexual abuse is when someone is touched, forced to take part in sexual acts, made to take their clothes off, photographed naked or partly clothed, or forced to look at inappropriate materials and pictures. Someone who sexually abuses children and young people is called a paedophile, and to make anyone under 16 do any of these things is a criminal offence. Nearly all people who sexually abuse children and young people are known and trusted by the victims themselves, and are often part of the family or close family friends.

Abuse is much more in the open than it used to be, but it's hard to say whether more teenagers are abused now than used to be the case. Some men are attracted to girls and will try to befriend or 'groom' girls in order to do some of the things mentioned above. You need to be aware of that and make sure that you're not normally on your own with older men you don't know too well. There is also a small number of women who like to initiate boys into sexual activity, and that is wrong too. Teenagers who have been abused in the past may be confused about what physical contact and sex is all about, and could feel guilty, used and worthless. God doesn't see it like that. He hates the pain that victims of abuse feel, and he wants to heal the feelings and memories. If anything like this has happened to you, remember that it is never your fault and you didn't cause it.

It is never right for anyone to be abused by someone else. If you are treated badly, asked to do anything you're not sure about or touched in a way that makes you feel uncomfortable, don't keep it a secret but tell an adult you trust.

Sexual Arousal

see also Foreplay, Petting, Sexual Intercourse

This is about being 'turned on' and is usually what happens in the run-up to sexual intercourse. Boys get aroused when they think of things, see pictures or have daydreams about girls, as well as when they're kissing and cuddling. You could be a real turn-on for your boyfriend, and he could get you excited too. You may also find pictures of attractive men and boys arousing. With your hormones helping you grow up and your excitement about the opposite sex, sexual arousal can be quite powerful and overwhelming, and that's a bit of a problem. If you get too aroused and you're in a position where you are getting intimate with your boyfriend, you could end up doing things you'll cringe about afterwards or which have really serious consequences. There's lots more in this book about this, so keep reading!

Sexual Intercourse

see also Boyfriends, Gay, Lesbian, Love, Masturbation, Sexual Arousal, Virgin

The act of sexual intercourse is the culmination of a great deal of relationship-building and is something that should be saved for marriage. Yet we are bombarded and surrounded by images of sex and stories in magazines, TV dramas and films that suggest that having sex is a great thing to do at any time and pretty well with anyone! Because sex is discussed so openly, we're all left with the impression that everyone is doing it except us! We cheapen it with slang words such as the F word, bonking or shagging.

Sex has got completely out of hand. People's 'need' for sex means that they use others rather than really love them. The ideal of sex between a man and a woman has got confused and rejected. Marriages have split up because one or other of the partners wanted more sex than the marriage offered. God didn't want it to be this way.

The act of sex or 'making love', when the man's erect penis enters the woman's vagina, should be a very special experience between two people of opposite genders who are formally committed to each other for life through marriage. This is the only way in which they can give to one another completely without feeling used or abused by the other. Many young people have had their understanding of what sex and love really mean ruined by rushing into it before they were ready and feeling cheap and messed up, and before the legal age of consent of 16. Young people who 'sleep around' are putting themselves in danger of catching a number of very nasty sexually transmitted diseases, risking pregnancy and the responsibility of parenthood, and suffering the pain of heartbreak and rejection time and time again. This can damage their emotional well-being not just for a while but for life.

Boys have the responsibility not to force a girl to do anything that she doesn't want to do or that you both know you shouldn't do. Girls have a responsibility to make sure that her boyfriend knows what he can and can't do, and not to lead him on and then want to stop when it's going too far. You also have to keep control of yourself and make sure that you're not going too far. Any girl who is forced into sexual activity has a right to report the boy, and in extreme cases this could be classed as rape.

Accidents can happen when cuddling goes further, so you need to be realistic about yourself and avoid situations where you could go too far. If you think you or he could get over-excited, avoid being on your own in private and be careful where your hands and his hands go. It's not easy to understand right now, but it is worth it to wait before you get into sexual activity.

Sexually Transmitted Diseases

see also Abstinence, Contraception, Sexual Activity, Sexual Intercourse

STDs, or sexually transmitted infections (STIs) as they're sometimes known, are on the increase amongst young people. In the UK there's been a 2 per cent increase in an already high rate of STDs, and the Health Protection Agency has warned that efforts to reduce these rates are being hampered by young people like you being bombarded with images and messages that encourage casual sex. Young people are at risk of getting an STD by having unprotected sex and by changing partners and sleeping around. Here's yet another reason why God's ideal is best! He wants us to keep ourselves clear of sexual intercourse until we have met our lifelong partner, so that we don't infect him or pick something up from him.

There's lots of information around on STDs and STIs in books, on websites and in sex education at school. Some can affect the girl alone, some can have long-term health risks and even cause a girl to become infertile, and some can be very painful and damaging for boys. Some of the STDs that affect girls are as follows:

Chlamydia doesn't always make itself known to girls – in fact, about 70 per cent can pass it on to boys without knowing they've got it! Once it flares up it leads to pain, bleeding and irregular periods. It can also cause internal damage that in the worst cases can lead to infertility.

Crabs or Pubic Lice are little crab-like blood-sucking parasites that are passed on through pubic hair touching during sex. They are painful, itchy and spread fast.

Gonorrhoea may cause a yellow discharge from the vagina or bum, bleeding and pain during and after sex, pain when weeing and a sore throat. It can be treated by medicine.

Genital Herpes lasts for about three weeks and can include itching and pain in the genital area, sores on the mouth and vaginal area, scabs, headaches and pain when weeing.

Many of these STDs, and others that are less common but often more serious, can be avoided by making sure you are clean and have good personal hygiene habits, and by not having sex until you're with the right person, at the right time, for life! It's simple – if young people didn't sleep around, have short-term sexual relationships and fail to protect themselves, then the rates of STDs would shrink dramatically!

Sperm

see Boys' Bits, Pregnancy

Suicide

see also Heartbreak, Lies, Rebellion

Suicide is simply when someone kills themself. There are lots of ways that people try this and many attempts at suicide fail. There is an alarming rise in the number of teenagers who attempt suicide, and in many cases succeed, and lots of stories and research about why this may be the case. Suicide is a major cause of teenage death and has increased dramatically over the past 25 years.

Many young people who have attempted suicide say that they didn't really want to die, but they simply couldn't see a way through their feelings. When a suicide attempt leads to death, the lives of all those around the young person – parents, brothers and sisters, wider family, friends, teachers, neighbours – are damaged and changed for life. Many will feel responsible and guilty, and they may never understand what happened and why.

You'll know that there's lots of pressure on you right now, and that pressure can sometimes seem too much. Maybe your body is changing, your emotions and feelings are mixed up, you're worried about your weight and appearance, you are being pressured to succeed at home and at school, and you've not got a boyfriend. When you're young, you may think that these situations will never go away, you feel down and depressed, and you think you may never be able to cope with them . . . but you will. God never gives us more than we can manage and is always there to help us get through and see his power through everything. Once you get through a rough patch, you start to realise that you can cope and things do get better!

Young people get depressed over many things, and relationships are one of the most likely causes. You may feel down because you're a bit confused about whether you fancy girls or boys, you may be upset because everyone else seems to have a boyfriend except you, or you may have been really hurt by a relationship that has gone wrong. When you're in the middle of these down times, it's hard to take the advice and support that others give, but it's always worth trying. Most people who've been through these times will remind you that the feelings you have will pass, new relationships will come along and you'll learn from the hard time you're going through.

Suicide is not God's plan for anyone. God's got a great life planned for everyone who trusts and follows him, and it's guaranteed to be better than any life we can plan without God involved! If you're feeling really depressed, get help, talk to anyone who will listen, and remember the key truth – God will help you whatever!

Tt

Tampons

see Periods

Teachers

see also Advice, Men

Teachers are there to help you! They may seem like they're from another planet but most of your teachers do care about you and your friends and are interested in how life in school and out of school is going for you. Teachers are good at offering advice and help if you need it, and there's probably nothing you can ask them that they've not been asked before! I know it can seem hard to believe but they were teenagers too, so they know something about what you're going through! If you're worried about relationships or want to know what to do about a tough situation, try asking a teacher you trust. Many teachers can be really helpful about how to cope with rejection by a boy and what to do to make yourself more attractive to them.

For some boys and girls as they grow up, teachers can become an object of desire! Some of the younger teachers may only be eight years older than you, and some young male teachers are attractive, with all the right bits in the right places! The problem is that the age gap is really huge and you don't stand a chance chasing a teacher. It's far better to learn about boys from those the same age as you, rather than setting your sights on a mature man you can never get. If a teacher does get into a relationship with a pupil, it is against the law as it is considered to be inappropriate and a form of sexual abuse, so they'll end up in huge trouble and probably lose their job. So look but don't touch – and thank God for the wonder of men!

Termination

see also Contraception, Pregnancy

Termination, also known as abortion, is always really sad and difficult for a woman or girl to cope with. Termination is when the life of an unborn child who is growing in the womb is ended deliberately by medical means. No pregnancy can be terminated if the child growing in the womb is more than 24 weeks old. There are some other strict laws and guidelines about it, and there are important considerations to be taken into account, including the health of the 'mother' and if the baby is likely to have significant physical problems when they're born.

Some people argue that termination is a good way out of the situation if a girl becomes pregnant unexpectedly, or has what is called an 'unwanted' pregnancy. But this argument forgets that when a girl is developing a life inside her, lots of things are happening to her emotions and hormones that are making her feel attached to the unborn child. It is very difficult and damaging to the future well-being of the mother for her developing child to be killed in the womb and disposed of, even if it is what the girl thinks she wants at the time. About 5 per cent of women who have terminations are never able to get pregnant again. The pro-abortion argument also assumes that any woman has a right to decide what happens to her own body, even if that means ending the life of an unborn child. Many Christians would argue that the growing child has rights too and that these shouldn't be ignored.

Most Christians are really concerned about abortion, particularly where young girls are involved. Human life is special and sacred, a great gift from God. We have to think through whether any people have the right to take the life of someone else, especially a helpless unborn child. To kill a developing child for our own convenience is a really selfish, irresponsible way to behave.

Some boys who get their girlfriends pregnant try to push them into having a termination because they don't want to take responsibility for a child. But that's also a really selfish attitude, and one that could scar and damage the girl for ever. It takes two to produce a child, and the boy has to take mature responsibility as well as the girl who carries it. No boy can simply walk away.

By far the best way to avoid this ever being an issue for you personally is to love and cherish your boyfriend, never go too far into sex until you're in a life-long relationship in marriage, don't be pressured by any boy or man, and learn about contraception.

Trust

see also Lies, Precious, Two-Timing

All relationships are based on trust. We know we can trust God because he always keeps his promises and we've seen and known God help us. But people can sometimes break the trust we place in them. You know what it's like when a close friend lets you down by spreading secrets about you that you trusted her to keep to herself. Trust is easily broken and quite hard to rebuild.

You and your boyfriend will need to reach a point of really trusting each other; otherwise the relationship isn't going to grow and isn't going to help either of you develop. You need to trust him with your feelings, hopes, plans, desires and frustrations. You'll need to trust him to keep things to himself and not to hurt you by rejecting you or having another girlfriend at the same time. In the same way he will be trusting you to love him, make him feel special, keep what he says and does between you and look after him. He will need to be able to trust you not to take advantage of him or manipulate him emotionally.

When trust in a relationship breaks down, it's not impossible to make a fresh start but it's not easy either. If you break the trust he's put in you, you'll be damaging him and revealing a really nasty side of yourself. You'll need to work hard to prove to him that he can trust you again.

Two-Timing

see also Lies, Trust

A few really selfish boys think it is fun to have two girlfriends at the same time, or men betray their wives by having an affair with someone else. Girls and women do the same too. Two-timing is about having two boyfriends and keeping each one secret from the other, pretending to love or care about each but really only caring about yourself! This is a sick way of treating people and something to be really ashamed of! There's no way a good relationship can develop when it is based on deception and lies, and inevitably boys will get hurt and feel used in the process. If you're tempted to two-time your lad, just imagine for a moment how you would feel if he did that to you . . . and think again!

Vv

Valentine's Day

see also Boyfriends, Give and Take, Love, Precious

Valentine's Day is a bit of a laugh and you shouldn't take it too seriously. It's a bit embarrassing seeing the cards your parents buy for each other, and it's a bit nerve-racking waiting to find out if you've been sent a Valentine!

If you have got a special lad in your life, don't forget to get him something a little special, but don't go overboard. Boys are less bothered about these things than girls. And if you find that he's got another Valentine card, don't get upset – just be proud that you have managed to catch a fit boy that another girl wants too!

There's a great deal of fuss made about this one day in February, but if you really do love a guy, then the way you show that you care for him every day is much more important than what you buy him on one day out of 365. And if he gets really upset because he's not been given a fantastic gift, then you may want to think whether he's the sort of guy you deserve. Love and affection are about what happens all the time, and if he's only after pressies, he's not really committed to you.

Whatever you get or give on Valentine's Day, it's what you are willing to give the rest of the time that matters. Love isn't about one day each February!

Virgin

see also Pregnancy, Sexual Intercourse, Sexually Transmitted Diseases

Although the word has been used to advertise all sorts of things from an airline to a brand of perfume, the word 'virgin' is really important and really powerful. If someone is a virgin, they have something to be really proud of and they're proving that they're not going to go along with the crowd. They have self-respect and know what they want. There's loads in the Bible about the value and importance God places on virginity: it is a sign of people who are not tempted, remain strong and trust him.

A virgin is simply someone who has not had sexual intercourse with someone else. A girl who is a virgin deserves respect and praise, and shouldn't be teased or bullied because of it. A virgin has decided not to get into sex too soon and is probably waiting for her life-partner to come along. She is not going to be used by boys, she is not going to be pressured by her peers and so-called 'friends', and she is going to keep the precious gift of her virginity for the one special boy at the right time.

Remaining a virgin is a sensible decision. The risks for girls of having sex too soon are much greater than those for boys, as girls are more susceptible to picking up sexually transmitted diseases, and they're the ones who could get pregnant if they have unprotected sex or the condom fails.

There's still a bit of a myth around that it's OK for boys to sleep around but not for girls. That's simply rubbish! If your boyfriend is a virgin, you should be really happy about it because it shows he's really something special. Many young people lie about whether they're a virgin or not, so don't be fooled by what they say . . . many have vivid imaginations!

Ww

Women

see also Girls, Girls' Bits, Equality, Pornography

Men and boys will never fully understand women and girls! Biologically and physically, women are smaller than men, carry more fat and have less muscle. Emotionally, you are often more sensitive, aware of how others feel and more able to express your feelings. There are some myths around about women which are probably not true . . . although you may know different! It is said that women talk more than men, that they spend longer in the bathroom and that they change their minds all the time. But there are boys who behave just the same!

Women are not made to be the slaves of men or children. Even in this enlightened age there are still a few situations in the workplace and in society where women are seen as being lower than men, probably because they have traditionally taken the leading role in giving up careers to look after children. God made us all equal.

Women, like teenage girls, face regular times of pain during their periods and may become moody and irritable for a few days. When this happens to you, you'll need a little space and some extra care.

Women are often abused by men. Many people would say that pornographic pictures of women posing naked is not how we should treat women – no one was created by God to be used in that way. There are also women who are prostitutes – women who sell sex to men, often because they are desperate for money. The men who use them are abusing them – and God hates it.

Yy

Young

see also Activities, Adolescence, Hormones

This may seem really obvious to you, but you're still young and there's no rush to get older. Most people who are older than you will tell you that they'd much rather be young again and be able to enjoy the life you lead. As tough as the teenage years are for you, life later will be tougher.

Don't strive to get older, behave as if you're older or rush into adult things. Make the most of the time you have during these precious years, enjoy yourself – and enjoy God's love for you.

Some contact addresses, phone numbers and websites

AIDS	National Aids helpline: (0800) 567123 www.thewellproject.org
Alcohol Abuse	Alcoholics Anonymous (AA), London helpline: (0171) 352 3001. Head Office, PO Box 1, Stonebow House, York YOI 7NJ. (01904) 644026 Alcohol Action Wales, 8th Floor, Brunel House, 2 Fitzlan Rd, Cardiff CF2 1EB www.alcoholics-anonymous.org
Childline	(0800)1111. Freepost 1111, London N1 ORR NSPCC Childline: (0800) 800500 www.ChildLine.co.uk
Christian Holidays and Mission Projects	Scripture Union: 207 – 209 Queensway, Bletchley, Milton Keynes MK2 2EB. Tel: (01908) 856000. Fax: (01908) 856111 www.scriptureunion.org.uk

Crusaders (Crusoe):
2, Romeland Hill, St. Albans, Herts
AL3 4ET

World Horizons, North Dock Centre,
Llanelli Dyfed.
www.worldhorizons.co.uk

Drug Abuse

Lifeline: (90161) 8392054

Re-Solv (Society for Prevention of
Solvent and Volatile Substance Abuse):
30a High St, Stone, Staffs ST15 8AW
www.drugfree.org

Eating Disorders

Youth Helpline: (01603) 765050
Mon – Fri, 4 – 6 pm

The Eating Disorder Association:
First Floor, Wensum House,
103 Prince of Wales Rd, Norwich,
Norfolk NR1 1DW. (01603) 621414

The Anorexia and Bulimia Nervosa
Association, Tottenham Women and
Health Centre Annexe, Tottenham,
London N15 4RK
www.nationaleatingdisorders.org

Giving up Smoking	Smoker's Quitline: Wales: (01222) 0641888 London: (0171) 4873000
	ASH (Action for Smoking and Health), 5-11 Mortimer Street, London W1A 4QW www.nhs.uk/gosmokefree
Pregnancy Advice	Care Centre Network: CARE (0800) 0282228 www.pregnancy.org.uk www.christiananswers.net/pregnancy

Nick Harding can be contacted through the publisher's address at the front of the book. He can also be found on Facebook!